The Encyclopedic Dictionary for Graphoanalysts

The Encyclopedic Dictionary for Graphoanalysts

COMPLETE AND UNABRIDGED

by the IGAS Department of Instruction

INTERNATIONAL GRAPHOANALYSIS SOCIETY

Chicago, Illinois, U. S. A.

FOREWORD

by the President of International Graphoanalysis Society, Inc.

More than three decades have passed since M.N. Bunker started teaching others the principles of handwriting analysis derived from his unique theories and observations. In the intervening years Graphoanalysis has not stood still. Mr. Bunker, himself, always continued searching and testing: searching for newer understandings and testing applications of old ideas. Since his death in 1961, a vigorous effort has been made by the International Graphoanalysis Society to further upgrade the professional status of Graphoanalysis. The effort has been successful.

This success is not due to one person or to one small group of people. It has come about through the work of many. These include the Home Office staff, which is continuing study and research to achieve a fuller understanding of the relationship between Graphoanalysis and psychology. It includes Society members at large who continue to bring to public notice the unique benefits Graphoanalysis offers in the fields of teaching, counseling, business, and law enforcement. It includes members who have specialized training or who work in the field of psychology, and who have voluntarily contributed hundreds of hours to contemporary scientific research in Graphoanalysis.

The publication of this ENCYCLOPEDIC DICTIONARY FOR GRAPHOANALYSTS, with its many specialized terms, definitions, stroke meanings, and illustrations, represents another step forward. It strengthens the status of Graphoanalysis as a profession. It clearly points to this particular discipline of handwriting analysis as a valid method of personality assessment.

Because of the eminent success of Graphoanalysis, you can be justifiably proud that you are a member of this profession.

V. PETER FERRARA

V

PREFACE

The **ENCYCLOPEDIC DICTIONARY FOR GRAPHO-ANALYSTS** was compiled for the express purpose of helping Graphoanalysts improve the effectiveness of their work, regardless of the field or fields in which they choose to specialize. It was written to serve both the student who has not yet completed his formal academic training in Graphoanalysis, and the member who needs supplementary vocabulary and review of fundamentals in order to produce an acceptable Graphoanalysis.

This volume was written with three specific objectives in mind:

The first objective is to make available for every Graphoanalyst, whether a beginner or an experienced graduate, a ready reference to help him solve specific problems in Graphoanalysis.

The second objective of this book is to enrich every Graphoanalyst's knowledge by providing a more comprehensive coverage of Graphoanalysis than has heretofore been available in any form.

For the last objective this volume has been thoroughly prepared in order to increase the professional stature of Graphoanalysis by providing a compilation of specialized terms and definitions relevant to this particular discipline of handwriting analysis.

Analyzing handwriting involves responsibility. That the Graphoanalyst can and must assume certain responsibilities in order to be a good analyst is evident. He must, first of all, be responsible for making an accurate evaluation of the strokes in the writing. He must be responsible for communicating clearly to another individual that which is revealed in the writing. He must assume the obligation to refrain from dulling the understanding of others by needless repetition of words or phrases. Use of the ENCYCLOPEDIC DICTIONARY can be a tremendous help to every Graphoanalyst in meeting these responsibilities.

The volume is divided into five parts: (1) the Foreword, by the President of International Graphoanalysis Society, Inc.; (2) the Preface; (3) Instructions on How to Use the ENCYCLOPEDIC DICTIONARY; (4) a completely alphabetized list of terms and definitions of traits (including explanations of how each trait is determined) with which every Graphoanalyst should become familiar; (5) a listing of 108 traits which are discussed in the General Course.

All terms in Part IV are identified as primary, evaluated, or both. The small letter *p* following the word indicates a primary trait, the small letter *e* an evaluated trait. When the word is followed by *ep*, it can be either primary or evaluated.

Specimens are series numbered rather than consecutively numbered. When referring to specimens, prefix the alphabetical letter to the specimen number for easier and more accurate identification.

HOW TO USE
THE ENCYCLOPEDIC DICTIONARY

1. For Solving Special Problems

When you prepare a Graphoanalysis, you are attempting to communicate with someone, orally or in writing. Whether or not you succeed in expressing your ideas so that that person can understand what you are saying depends upon your terminology. He cannot comprehend your meaning unless you first have a clear picture, an accurate conception of the meaning in your own mind.

If you are unsure of the exact meaning of a word you wish to use in a Graphoanalysis, especially the meaning applicable in a specific case, simply turn to that word in the ENCYCLOPEDIC DICTIONARY. It will be easy to find, because all terms are in alphabetical order.

For instance, do you hold the common misconception that the word *abnormal* always has an unfavorable connotation? It does not, as you will discover when you look up the word in the ENCYCLOPEDIC DICTIONARY. Positive traits as well as negative traits may exist in individuals to an abnormally high degree. Therefore, you may find evidences of abnormally strong positive characteristics in an individual's handwriting also.

Look up every word about which you have any doubts— and also those words about which you think you are sure. The same thing applies if you are in doubt about the stroke or strokes that reveal a certain trait. Turn to that term in the ENCYCLOPEDIC DICTIONARY.

When you locate the descriptive word, you will find thereupon whether the term is primary, evaluated, or both. You will learn what to look for in the writing to determine whether or not that term is evident. You will find many of the words illustrated in original specimens of handwriting. Numbers of these specimens were taken directly from the files of a counseling psychologist who verified the existence of the specified trait in the writer's personality.

VIII

You cannot use the same terminology with all people and expect them to understand what you are talking about. In a learning situation (which all Graphoanalysts are attempting to achieve when they give a Graphoanalysis) the learner perceives the situation from his own personal frame of reference. His capacity to understand is limited by his experience and his intelligence.

The chances are that a child—or an adult with a limited vocabulary—would see no meaning in perfectly useful words such as *petulant* or *vapid*. It is much more likely that the words *peevish* or *dull* would have some significance to him. Reference to your ENCYCLOPEDIC DICTIONARY, where such synonyms are found, can furnish many opportunities to tailor your Graphoanalyses to fit the client.

Graphoanalysts often find themselves in the position of having to prepare Graphoanalyses for different members of the same family or of giving short oral analyses to members of a group. In such cases, repetition of the same name for a trait or repetition of the same descriptive adjectives is not good. It leads to skepticism of your ability to differentiate between individual personalities—and it is boring. How do you avoid this tiresome habit? Refer to your ENCYCLOPEDIC DICTIONARY. Numerous synonyms and cross-references are available for this purpose.

Look up *warmhearted*, for instance. Read what is said about it. Are there not many times when examination of a handwriting specimen would warrant your use of this term in place of the hackneyed expression, "Your writing indicates that you have a *sympathetic nature*"?

No one is so well educated or so well informed that he does not need to refer to a dictionary at times. No one has gained so much knowledge of Graphoanalysis that he can fail to benefit from turning to his ENCYCLOPEDIC DICTIONARY for specific information and help.

2. To Enrich Your Knowledge of Graphoanalysis

This volume is not intended as a replacement in any way of the General or Graduate Courses in Graphoanalysis. It is rather to be considered as a supplement to provide additional information; to help you correct careless habits or erroneous procedures in analyzing handwriting; to give you new insights in evaluating traits, particularly in evaluating trait combinations; and to broaden your knowledge of Graphoanalysis as a profession, as a science.

If you are a Graphoanalyst who studied the General Course some time ago, or one who has forgotten much of what you learned, you can virtually re-educate yourself by studying (and applying) the interpretations found in this ENCYCLOPEDIC DICTIONARY. Principles covered in the General Course are included in clear, concise form, but much, much more than basic principles is included.

Simply by thumbing through these pages you will find numbers of original handwriting specimens. In many instances, a brief part of the writer's case history is presented along with the description of the trait exemplified. Give yourself a refresher course in Graphoanalysis by studying the specimens and the descriptions preceding them.

Besides finding the applicable definition given for each word in the ENCYCLOPEDIC DICTIONARY, you will often find that more than one meaning for the word is involved. For example, *individualism* has two distinctly different interpretations in ordinary dictionaries. Perhaps the only meaning you associated heretofore with this word (in Graphoanalysis) was the one pertaining to an individual peculiarity or idiosyncrasy. Perhaps it never occurred to you to use this word in reference to a writer who shows extreme independence of thought and action by his short *t* and *d* stems. Yet, as you learned in your textbooks, such a writer will live his life in his own way without regard for the opinions of others. One meaning of *individualism* is "the living of one's life in one's own way without regard for others."

Another way to enrich your knowledge of and increase your skill in the field of Graphoanalysis is to leaf through the pages of the ENCYCLOPEDIC DICTIONARY and note the terms having neither *p, e,* nor *ep* after them. Do you ever use the word "always" in making an analysis? Watch out! Look this word up in the ENCYCLOPEDIC DICTIONARY. Scientific psychologists guard against using absolutes in descriptions of human behavior. Graphoanalysts must use this same caution in order to achieve a truly professional status.

The above examples are typical of the valuable supplementary material to be found in this book. Remember, though, that all of the new information to be found here has not changed the basic principles of Graphoanalysis; it has merely added to that which was already available.

This ENCYCLOPEDIC DICTIONARY FOR GRAPHO- ANALYSTS provides Graphoanalysts with a realistic, down-to-earth, yet academically and psychologically sound compendium of knowledge in the area of Graphoanalysis up to the present time. It offers you a springboard from which you can dive more deeply into the waters of awareness. If it helps you to help yourself to become a better Graphoanalyst, it will have achieved its purpose.

The
Encyclopedic
Dictionary
for
Graphoanalysts

A

ABERRANT *e* Deviating from what is normal or typical. To use this adjective in an analysis the Graphoanalyst must first be familiar with the writing of many persons. It is necessary to know to what extent a trait appears on the average (i.e., in approximately two-thirds of the general population) in order to determine whether or not the writer is prone to either mental or emotional aberrations.

ABILITY *ep* Every individual who can write possesses the power to do something, physical or mental, but everyone does not have a special talent in a particular field such as art, music, or literature. For examples of primary traits indicating special ability, look under artistic ability, literary ability, etc. To arrive at any conclusion about the ability of a writer to do a particular type of work, affirmative and negative traits must all be taken into consideration.

There are indications of many different abilities in this specimen of writing, which was done by a brilliant college student. There are also indications of traits that may be considered liabilities rather than assets. The points on the *m's* and *n's* show the keenness of his exploratory mind; the frequent breaks between the letters of words show his ability to appreciate and understand music; the short *d* and *t* stems show his ability to think and act independently; the tie loop on *f's* and *s* show persistence, the ability to stick to a job. This is a partial list of traits indicating ability in this writing. On the other hand, the majority of his *t* crossings are to the left of the *t* stem; the habit of procrastination will not help him fulfill his potential. Self-consciousness and inhibitions are

3

also evident. The former is shown when the last part of *m* or *n* is higher than the first part; the latter, in the re-traced, squeezed lower portions of the *h*.

There is no doubt as to whether or not this writer has ability. Other traits, however, will determine to what extent he will fulfill his potentialities.

Just as care fully give examination, have a path of passivity an obedience to the seem

Specimen 1

ABJECT *p* All intensely expressive people will feel miserable and wretched at times. When the writing has the far forward slant, you know the writer will often undergo such phases of emotional reaction.

this take to

Specimen 2

ABLE *ep* Whether an individual has much power of the mind is determined not only by the type of thinker his writing shows him to be; psychologists have learned that his intelligence is highly correlated with such positive traits as persistence, determination and conscientiousness. Evaluation is necessary. In the case of the talented person, his special gift may be shown as a primary trait such as a good sense of color or creative ability. Again, before any prediction can be made as to the likelihood of his fulfilling his potential, all of the evidence of the strokes in the writing must be weighed.

ABNORMAL, ABNORMALLY *e* Not normal; not average. Normal is generally used by psychologists to refer to that which is typical of two-thirds of the population. Both positive and negative traits may appear in handwriting to an abnormally high degree, so abnormal does not necessarily have an unfavorable connotation. The average or normal person may be sensuous but not sensual; therefore, heavy, blotted, and corrugated writing indicates excessive sensuousness which can be considered abnormal.

Most people do not make *p* loops as inflated as the writer of this specimen. Thus it can be judged that he has an abnormally strong mental desire for physical activity.

These are the people
per se for they

Specimen 3

ABORTIVE *e* Evidence of talent that comes to nothing, is fruitless or unsuccessful, is usually accompanied by an absence of positive supporting traits such as determination (shown by heavy downstrokes), purpose (shown by heavy *t* bars), and definiteness (shown by blunt finals).

ABOVEBOARD *p* Without dishonesty or concealment. The person who is open and aboveboard will write circle letters with neither initial nor final loops. The circles may be open or closed at the top as long as the closure is not looped.

Specimen 4

ABRUPT *ep* The person who is sudden and short in behavior or speech will show this by blunt finals to strokes in his handwriting and there will be an absence of evidence of diplomacy. This characteristic is frequently accompanied by frankness or talkativeness.

Specimen 5

ABSENT-MINDED *e* Light *t* bars written well above the stem indicate the daydreamer. Absence of *i* and *j* dots and *t* crossings show a lack of attention to what one is

6

doing; the mind is concerned with some matter other than the process of writing the words. Large, sprawling script may indicate aimless wandering of the mind. On the other hand, very small writing shows a total concentration of attention so that the writer would be absorbed in what he is doing to the extent that he might be considered absent-minded, especially if he is so preoccupied that he cannot readily turn his attention to something new.

ABSOLUTE. Not dependent on anything else; considered without reference to anything else. There are no absolutes in Graphoanalysis. No one single stroke can ever be considered absolute evidence of the extent to which the writer has a trait without taking into consideration the effect other traits will have on it. The writer who makes heavy *t* crossings that show a strong sense of purpose cannot be considered to have a very strong will power should his downstrokes below the line be light and short, as this reveals weak determination. In the usual dictionary sense, will power and determination are synonymous, although in Graphoanalysis will power is interpreted as purpose or setting of goals, and determination refers to the force of will that is put into carrying out goals or purposes.

ABSOLUTIST *ep* Characterized by absolutism; despotism, certainty, positivism. Look for extremely blunt, definite finals; they may frequently be accompanied by the strong, blunt *t* crossings showing the dominating personality.

Specimen 6

ABSORPTIVE *p* This is used in relation to the ability of the individual to absorb, to assimilate, emotional experiences, and is shown by the width or heaviness and depth of strokes. The heavy line writer who has a far forward slant not only absorbs emotional experience but also expresses his emotional reactions to it, thus relieving himself of some of the weight of the emotional situation as he is affected by it. But the person who has this deep capacity for making an emotional experience an enduring part of his psychological make-up without having the ability to express his emotional reaction to it, can be considered truly absorptive. He may carry the effects of a traumatic experience in childhood the rest of his life, in spite of conscious efforts to forget it. Such a writer is a middle-aged man who is repulsed by any form of dressing an animal to prepare it for food. This repulsion goes back to his reactions to seeing a cat skinned when he was three years old.

Where it is now

Specimen 7

ABSORPTIVITY *p* The quality of being absorptive. See ABSORPTIVE.

ABSTEMIOUS *e* Not self-indulgent. This will be shown by the absence of desire for self-gratification. The writing will be light; there will be no signs of sensuousness or sensuality.

ABSTINENT *e* Practicing abstaining from or the doing without some particular pleasure. This voluntary doing without may require self-control as typified by bow-like *t* bars and strong will power. Some writers may show that they abstain from making close personal friendships because of their natures; this is shown by the small, squared lower loops that indicate clannishness.

ABSTRACT IMAGINATION *p* The power of creating mental images that are apart from the material or the practical; the ability to understand ideas and theories created by others, as in philosophy. This is determined in the upper loop letters (aside from *d* and *t*); the larger and higher the loops, the greater is the imagination.

It is not surprising that the writer of Specimen 8 is majoring in philosophy rather than in a more practical field such as business administration. Note the difference in the size of the upper loops in comparison to the lower ones.

Specimen 8

9

ABUSIVE *e* The person who hurts others by treating them badly or by speaking harshly to them will frequently show in his writing a combination of sarcasm and the desire to domineer. Other negative traits that may also be present are temper, vanity and excessive outspokenness.

ACCEPT, ACCEPTANCE. The principles of Graphoanalysis are based on taking willingly into account all facets of human nature and of dealing with them objectively, without bias or prejudice. Graphoanalysts accept every human individual.

ACCOMMODATING *e* Having a willing disposition; obliging. This can be determined by a combination of various traits such as generosity (long finals on words), desire for responsibility (large initial circle loops, particularly on capitals), and yielding strokes (as in the sprawled *s*). There will be an absence of such negative traits as resentment and selfishness.

ACCUMULATIVE *e* There will be both acquisitiveness and conservativeness shown in the writing, but expenditure traits will not be in evidence.

Specimen 9 consistently shows the initial acquisitive hook, conservative spacing of the letters, and no long finals to indicate generosity.

other students and do something along

Specimen 9

10

ACCURATE *e* This characteristic is revealed not only in the careful dotting of *i's* and *j's*, but also in precise *t* crossings and in careful and exact formation of all letters.

after seeing this
decided that it

Specimen 10

ACERBITY *e* Sharpness and harshness of temper or words may be shown in combinations of sarcasm, temper, irritability, tendency to domineer, resentment, outspokenness and critical thinking. It is often due to bitterness resulting from deep emotion or intense emotional reactions.

ACQUIESCENT *e* The individual who accepts or consents without protest will show yielding strokes as in the sprawling, rounded, unformed *s*. Other traits in evidence may be desire to conform to socially acceptable standards, weak will power, indecisiveness, diplomacy, and a sympathetic or emotionally responsive nature. There will be an absence of indications of aggressiveness, domination and bluntness.

The girl who wrote Specimen 11 was described by her professors as a "mousy" type of person who would go along with anything suggested by others. Weak will power is shown in the weak *t* crossings; note the yielding tendency of the *s's*; the retraced *d's* and *t's* show the desire to conform to socially acceptable standards; diplomacy is shown in the way the letters get smaller at the end of words such as accurate; the emotional slant shows her sympathetic nature.

11

ct, the cave men who
years ago must have
they drew accurate
n the walls of their

ACQUISITIVE *p* Eager to acquire. That which is acquired may be accumulated or it may be given to others; the desire to possess means only to acquire, regardless of later usage. It is determined by initial hooks before letters or strokes. Although these hooks are most easily noticed at the beginning of a word, they are also found at the beginning of a stroke within a word. The size of the hook in relation to other strokes determines the type of value desired. Small hooks indicate the desire of all things; large hooks indicate the desire for large possessions or values, such as fame.

This can now
just cabout

ACRID, ACRIMONIOUS *e* The writer who is bitter or caustic in speech may show such traits in his writing as sarcasm, temper, vanity, frankness and critical thinking.

ACRITICAL *e* When there is no tendency to criticism or critical judgment there will likely be no analytical ability, exploratory thinking, resentment, or independence of thought. Many of the same traits that characterize the acquiescent nature are likely to be evident in the writing.

ACTIVE, ACTIVITY *ep* The mentally active person, one who enjoys mental activity, is indicated by the pointed exploratory and the sharp comprehension strokes as found in *m*, *n*, *h*, and *r*. Supporting evidence is found in traits such as initiative, aggressiveness, determination and persistence. Desire for physical activity is shown in large *p* loops, but whether or not the writer is active physically is influenced by his actual physical ability to satisfy that desire. Large lower and upper loops that reach into the line of writing above or below show desire for mental or physical activity; in case of such lower loops (with the exception of *p* loops), the desire is based on love of change and variety.

The writer of Specimen 13 was a young woman who was an excellent student. The points in her *m*, *n*, and *h* are significant. Her persistence is shown in the tie loops of *s*, *p*, *t*, and *f*. Her activity was not confined to academic lines; she participated in all sports available at the school she attended. Both *p* loops are inflated, with the second one extending almost into the writing below it.

my special projee
to go farther in

Specimen 13

ACUITY, ACUMEN *p* Keenness of thought is shown in strokes in *m*, *n*, *h*, etc. when a needle-like point is formed. The deeper and sharper the point, the sharper the insight of the writer is.

Specimen 14 was written by an honor student in college. This can easily be understood by looking at the points on his *n's* and *h*, since there is a positive correlation between grades and native intelligence.

plants and rippling
the dangers of living

Specimen 14

ADAMANT *e* The writing of the unyielding individual will reveal such traits as stubbornness, strong will power, determination, persistence, and definiteness. There will be no sign of indefiniteness. This adjective can most frequently be applied to the poised, cool person, as the emotionally responsive one is too easily swayed by emotional appeals.

This writer (Specimen 15) was considered adamant by his friends. The lack of emotional responsiveness is shown in the slant, which in most cases is straight up and down. The *t* in the second line indicates stubbornness, with a tendency toward it in the *d*. His definiteness is evident through the blunt endings of final strokes in "through," "the," and "orientated."

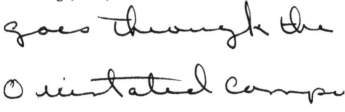

Specimen 15

ADAPTABLE, ADAPTABILITY *e* Several things must be taken into consideration in determining whether or not the writer is able to adjust easily to new circumstances. Rapidity and fluidity of thinking enable one to comprehend, to understand, new situations. Desire for change signifies a favorable attitude toward new situations. A sympathetic nature and an active imagination are helpful. Adaptability may result from a lack of definiteness, from a plastic, yielding nature. Traits that hamper the ability to adapt are self-consciousness, stubbornness, narrowmindedness, inhibition, etc.

ADDLE-BRAINED *e* This refers not only to a stupid person, but can also mean a muddled or confused one. Changeable slant, accompanied by confusion of upper and lower loops, showing confusion of interests, lack of ability to concentrate, general formlessness of the

15

writing—all of these may indicate an addle-brained person. All trait indications must be considered.

The writer of Specimen 16 was considered addle-brained not only by her professors, but also by her peer group. Note the changeable slant, undirected imagination (in the unfinished loops), lack of comprehension points in the *n*, and the extreme confusion of interests.

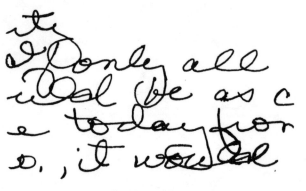

Specimen 16

ADMINISTRATIVE, ADMINISTRATOR *e* To be a good executive or manager requires intelligence, definiteness, will power, determination, imagination, organizational ability, persistence—in fact, almost any positive trait can be an asset to an administrator.

Specimen 17 is a sample of hurried writing done by a highly successful high school principal. Even though some of the points of the *m's* and *n's* are not sharp because of the speed with which this was written, there are still enough sharp points to indicate the mental ability of the writer. There is strong, lasting determination in the downstrokes of the *g* and *y's*. Analytical ability is shown in the *v* formations in *m* (second line) and *n* (third line). Some active imagination is evident: practical in the first *y* and philosophical in the loop of the *h* in "where." There were a number of loops showing philosophical imagination in the complete page of writing. Most of the final strokes are definite enough to indicate decisiveness.

Specimen 17

ADOLESCENT *e* Immature; lacking in definite formation of thoughts; lacking in emotional control. Some children show greater definiteness of purpose and greater emotional maturity in their writing than do many grown men and women.

ADVENTUROUS *e* In the adventurous person's writing will frequently be found love of change and variety (long lower loops), enthusiasm (long *t* crossings) aggressiveness, visionary goal setting, and independence. There will be a lack of caution and conservatism.

AESTHETE *e* Sensitivity to art and beauty may be revealed in a good sense of color (heavy writing), a good

17

sense of line values, philosophical imagination, intuitive-
ness (frequent breaks between the letters of words), and
a desire for culture (shown in the Greek *E*).

AFFABLE *e* First of all, the person who is easy to approach
and talk to will have either a sympathetic nature or be
emotionally responsive; he will often be generous, frank
and uninhibited. He will be neither irritable nor
domineering.

AFFECTATION *e* Artificial behavior meant to impress
others is determined by ostentatious writing: exaggerated
flourishes, capitals very large in relation to the rest of
the writing. Indications of vanity frequently accompany
this.

AFFECTIONATE *e* This personality trait has a high correlation with emotional responsiveness and generosity.
There will be an absence of negative traits that limit
expression, such as suppression, conservatism and secretiveness.

AFFLICTION *e* Both physical or mental suffering and
senility are revealed in corrugated, shaky writing. At
the present time there have not been enough scientifically
conducted experiments by Graphoanalysts for one to be
able to accept specific hypotheses as to exactly what the
writer's affliction may be.

The corrugations and shakiness of Specimen 18 are
due to senility, although the eighty-four year old woman
who wrote it is also suffering from heart trouble.

AGGRANDIZE *e* Those who make things seem greater than they are often have vanity, active imagination, desire to attract attention, and talkativeness.

AGGRAVATING *e* An annoying or vexing person may show negative traits like stubbornness, sarcasm, irritability, narrow-mindedness, temper, or a desire to domineer.

AGGRESSIVE *ep* This has two different connotations for use by Graphoanalysts. In a derogatory sense it implies a ruthless desire to dominate; in a favorable sense it means full of enterprise and initiative. Energetic pursuit of goals, invasion of new fields of activities, is indicated by basic strokes as in *p*, *g*, and *y* (see Specimen 19) when there is a strong forward swing of the upstroke away from the downstroke of the letter.

Specimen 19

AGILITY *e* May be mental or physical. Mental agility is shown by sharp exploratory or keen comprehension strokes in *m, n, h, r,* etc. This is often backed up by evidence of fluidity of thought. For physical agility one first must have the desire for physical activity supported by good coordination. The latter is often expressed in a good sense of rhythm, when the strokes come back to the base line with even spaces between the stroke combinations. Physical agility is, of course, contingent upon physical conditions making it possible for the writer to engage in physical activity. An invalid confined to a wheelchair can still have a strong mental desire for physical activity, even though agility is impossible.

AGITATION *e* This can be deduced from extreme variation in emotional reactions, shown by a slant that swings from one side of the scale to the other. There is also bound to be some emotional disturbance when the writing shows deep repression. The intensely responsive emotional

20

nature will naturally have intervals of tremulous excitement.

AGREEABLE *e* Shown by yielding strokes, sympathetic nature, conformity; there will be an absence of irritability and temper.

AIMLESS *p* The individual who has no definite aim or purpose is indicated by *t* bars placed very low on the *t* stems and made with light strokes

The student who wrote Specimen 20 is described by her professors as one who just drifts along. All *t* crossings are light in comparison to the rest of the writing and they are placed well down on the stem of the *t*, indicating no strong sense of purpose and no ambition.

Specimen 20

ALCOHOL. Writing done when the writer is under the influence of alcohol shows the same changes in personality characteristics that the individual shows. Many times one who is normally inhibited will, when intoxicated, lose much of his inhibitions; a normally timid person can become aggressive, etc. The writing reflects these changes, even though they are temporary.

ALTRUISTIC *e* One who is motivated by unselfish concern for the welfare of others will have some forward slant to his writing; it may range from B up to E. He will be generous and sympathetic. He will lack vanity or strong desire for self-gratification.

Specimen 21 is the writing of a man who spends much time on working with organizations like the Mental Health Association, Child Guidance Clinic, and Boy Scouts. He is highly motivated by the desire to help others; he would literally give the shirt off his back to anyone who was in need of it. His sympathetic nature is shown in the slant; his generosity is shown in the long finals.

Specimen 21

ALWAYS. Avoid using this word in a Graphoanalysis. Scientific psychologists must, because of the unpredictable element in human behavior, guard against the use of absolutes in describing or predicting the behavior of any individual or any group of individuals. Graphoanalysts must use this same caution.

AMATORY *e* The emotionally responsive person who lacks reticence and inhibitions is going to show his love--all of of his emotions, in fact.

AMBIDEXTROUS. Whether or not a person is able to use both hands with equal ease has no effect on the basic traits that will appear in his writing. Since writing is an expressive movement, directed by the brain, character-istics of the writer are revealed regardless of which hand holds the pen.

22

AMBIGUOUS. Graphoanalysts should avoid unclear, indefinite, uncertain or vague words and phrases when making any kind of personality assessment. Since basic personality traits are common in some degree to everyone, it is advisable to learn to evaluate characteristics in relation to the average; i.e., the extent to which the trait exists in two thirds of the population. To be quantitative rather than qualitative, the skilled Graphoanalyst judges whether or not the writer possesses a trait to the extent that the average person does or whether he possesses it to a greater or lesser degree than the average. The indefinite statement, "You are generous," is not significant enough to be considered scientifically accurate, as some generosity exists in most people in this culture. "Your generosity far exceeds that of the average individual," is more meaningful.

AMBITIOUS *e* A combination of high goals (crossings placed high on the *t* stems) and acquisitiveness (initial hooks) points to one who desires to achieve something, as fame, power or wealth.

Although the crossings (in Specimen 22) on the *t's* are high enough to be considered to indicate visionary goals, they are strong enough and long enough to indicate that the writer has enough enthusiasm and strength of purpose to achieve those goals. Acquisitiveness is indicated in the initial hook before express and the initial hook on the first *t* crossing.

Specimen 22

23

AMENABLE *e* One who is willing to follow advice is determined by yielding strokes (submissiveness), a responsive nature, and broadmindedness.

AMIABLE *e* Having a pleasant disposition. There will be an absence of signs of irritability or temper. The writer will have a sympathetic or emotionally responsive nature.

ANALYTICAL *p* The analytical type of mind is one capable of sifting or separating ideas and facts learned and determining the values and weaknesses of them. Analytical ability is synonymous with reasoning ability and is one of the components of intelligence. It may be found as an adjunct to the comprehensive, investigatory, or logical type of mind, and adds to the determination of the intelligence of the writer. Although it is most frequently in evidence in *m's* and *n's* (see Specimen 23), all *v* formations at the base line indicate analytical ability.

Specimen 23

ANTAGONISTIC *ep* This represents a hostile attitude toward others any may be deduced from strokes showing resentment of imposition, domineering tendencies, sensitivity to criticism, and vivid imagination.

Resentment of imposition is indicated by the straight, inflexible strokes before the first three words in Specimen 24; the domineering tendency is shown in the arrow-like *t* crossings that slant downward; sensitivity to criticism is evident in the looped *d* and *t*; an active imagination is shown in the loop of the *y*.

24

what did you think

Specimen 24

ANTIPATHETIC *ep* Synonym of antagonistic.

APATHETIC *e* Writing of an indifferent, unemotional, listless individual is characterized by lack of emotional responsiveness and of strokes showing determination, will power, ambition, or drive.

APTITUDE *e* A natural tendency; an ability; talent; quickness to learn or understand. Vocational aptitude can be determined solely by taking into consideration both the requirements for success in the vocation, and the personality pattern revealed by all traits, positive and negative, that are present in the handwriting.

ARDENT *e* Intensely enthusiastic; passionate. This can be determined from heavy line writing plus long, heavy *t* crossings as illustrated in Specimen 25.

d that hit

Specimen 25

25

ARGUMENTATIVE *e* This frequently involves analytical ability, talkativeness, irritability, sarcasm, stubbornness, impulsiveness and resentfulness.

ARROGANT *e* Full of unwarranted pride and self-importance. Pride to the extent of vanity will be present; this is evidenced by the very tall *t* and *d* stems. It will often be accompanied by a backward slant indicating self-interest, the arrow-like downward pointed *t* bars showing the tendency to domineer, and the ornate flourishes of ostentation.

ARTFUL *e* Skillful or clever, especially in getting what one wishes; deceitful. There will be evidence of deceit and fast thinking, particularly when diplomatic ability is strong.

ARTISTIC *e* Done skillfully; aesthetically satisfying. Artistic writing (shown in Specimen 26) involves graceful lines, accuracy of outline, color sense and absence of ostentation.

Specimen 26

ARTISTIC ABILITY *e* There are so many different forms of creative work (drawing, painting, sculpture, ceramics, and architecture) that are included in fine arts that "artistic ability" covers a very wide field. Traits to be considered in this broad category are color sense, heavy line writing; creative ability, broad topped *m's*, *n's* and *r's*; and a good sense of line values, graceful lines. Other

26

traits must be taken into consideration as they add to or detract from the evidence of the aforementioned traits.

ASCETIC *e* Self-denying; austere. This is evidenced by light strokes, showing the absence of strong appetites; by self-control, the bow shaped *t* bars; by love of simplicity and lack of ostentation.

ASPERITY *p* Sharpness of temper. It is determined by pointed bars that are made to the right of the *t* stem rather than across it. Irritability (jabbed *i* and *j* dots) and the tick stroke add weight to the evidence.

The tick stroke in Specimen 27, showing temper, is the short initial inflexible stroke on the *w*'s.

wind did that

Specimen 27

ASSET *ep* Any positive trait that is not carried to the extreme is considered a valuable or desirable thing to have. For example, enthusiasm, self-confidence, and determination are usually considered assets, but may be liabilities when carried to the extreme, as in a person who is overly enthusiastic, overly self-confident or overly determined.

ATHLETIC. Whether or not a person is physically skillful or active cannot be determined from his handwriting alone. However, the mental desire for physical activity is shown in inflated *p* loops. It is possible for one to be an active participant in sports requiring physical skill without its being based on this mental desire. Such parti-

27

cipation can be motivated by aggression, desire for fame, etc.

Specimen 28 shows a writer who does have a desire to be athletic.

Specimen 28

AUDACIOUS *e* Daring, reckless, bold. It can be determined through aggressiveness or initiative, self-reliance, independence, impulsiveness, and fast thinking. It is the opposite of timid.

AUSTERE *e* Very simple; lacking ornament. One who likes simplicity has no superfluous strokes in his penmanship. Many letters that are ordinarily considered loop letters will consist of only a stem. Light line writing and conservatism are likely to be present.

The author of Specimens 29 and 30 changed her slant on the page of writing, but that does not affect the extreme simplicity shown in the *t's, b's,* and *h.*

Specimen 29

to be confusing I will change
I don't use this one quite as

Specimen 30

AUTHENTICATE. Prove to be genuine. One of the facets of Graphoanalysis is the thorough development of skill and accuracy of observation so that a signature or other writing can be established as true or, on the contrary, as forged.

AUTOCRATIC *p* Synonym for domineering.

AVARICIOUS *e* This has a connotation of both greediness and miserliness. It is therefore determined by pronounced evidence of acquisitiveness along with extreme conservatism--no generosity whatever.

AVERAGE. When personality characteristics are assessed by Graphoanalysis, the term average is used to imply conformity with what is regarded as normal or ordinary, i.e., the extent to which a characteristic has been found to appear in the majority of the population.

B

BACKWARD *e* When using the meaning, shy, the evaluation rests on the same stroke combinations as timid. For the connotation of retarded, slow, there will be lack of investigative, analytical and comprehension strokes, lack of definiteness and other positive traits.

BAD. No single trait, standing alone, can be considered bad: this adjective has no place in the vocabulary of a Graphoanalyst. Whether a trait is a liability or an asset can be determined only through taking into consideration its combination with all other characteristics shown in the writing.

BEHAVIORISM. A doctrine of psychology formulated by John B. Watson and supported by many psychologists, which is contradictory to the theory on which Graphoanalysis is based. Behaviorists believe that overt or observed behavior provides the only valid data of psychology; the concept of mind is rejected. According to Graphoanalysis, handwriting is brain writing, revealing personality characteristics that cannot always be observed in overt behavior.

BELLICOSE *e* Of a quarrelsome or hostile nature: belligerent. The person with a chip on his shoulder will show in his writing much resentment. This is indicated by straight, inflexible initial strokes that lead from the base line up to the first letter of a word (or a combination of strokes) when that letter does not normally require such an initial stroke. There will also often be found in the writing sensitivity to criticism, talkativeness, irritability or temper, and vanity.

BENIGN *e* Good natured: kindly. Traits to look for include a sympathetic or responsive nature, generosity, broadmindedness; lack of irritability, temper, bluntness, domineering tendency, etc.

BIASED *ep* Prejudiced: partial. Anyone with a highly emotionally reactive nature will be biased to some extent because of the difficulty of viewing things objectively.

Bias will be enhanced by narrow-mindedness, shown in narrow *e's, o's, a's,* and *g's.*

The young man who wrote Specimen 1 was so biased in his perception of his own personality that even when there was agreement between standardized personality tests and assessment by a Graphoanalyst, he would not admit to possessing traits that he considered to be un-desirable. Note the narrowness of most of the circle letters (*a, e,* and *o*).

Specimen 1

BIGOTED *ep* Narrow-minded: prejudiced. Refer to biased above.

BLUFF, BLUFFER *ep* A person who misleads by a false, bold front writes with exaggeratedly wide and short, blunt downstrokes. There will frequently be in combination with this show of bluff such traits as outspokenness and deceit, ostentation and vanity.

BLUNT *ep* This is a synonym of bluff, but it implies a candor and tactlessness that show little regard for another's feelings. It is an antonym for diplomatic, so there will be no indications of diplomacy in the writing.

BOASTFUL *e* This is determined when many of the circle letters (*a, o,* and *g*) are left wide open at the top (talkativeness) and the *t* and *d* stems are so high in relation to the other letters that they indicate vanity. There will likely be irrelevant flourishes indicating ostentation.

BOLD *e* The fearless, audacious writer will often show aggressiveness, marked with self-reliance (strong underscores), and great determination. His writing will not show timidity, conservatism or inhibitions.

BORING *e* Dull, uninteresting, monotonous. This trait may be due to over-talkativeness, lack of comprehension, lack of imagination, boastfulness, or lack of interest in others.

BOSSY *p* Domineering, determined by arrow-like *t* bars (see Specimen 2) slanted downward.

Specimen 2

BOUNTIFUL *p* One who lacks restraint in giving will have long final strokes on the ends of words and broad spacing between letters and words.

The young man who wrote Specimen 3 was noted for his willingness to give of himself or his belongings. It was not impulsive giving, as he could always be counted on to share open-heartedly with others

Specimen 3

BRAGGART *e* An offensively boastful person. This is revealed by the same characteristics that are listed under boastful, but they will be even more marked.

BRASH *e* Too hasty in acting or speaking. This is usually based on impulsiveness, self-deceit and/or talkativeness.

BRAWNY. This is a physical attribute that cannot be determined by handwriting analysis. A puny individual who is definite, who possesses strong will power, determination, and other positive mental characteristics, will have a more forceful handwriting than will a strong, muscular person who is lacking in such positive attributes.

BRIGHT *e* This is a synonym of intelligent and is determined not only by the rapidity of thinking, the keenness of comprehension of the writer, but also by correlated traits such as persistence, determination, ability to concentrate, and definiteness.

BRILLIANT *ep* The keenly intelligent person is revealed by the sharp, pointed strokes on *m, n, r,* etc. plus correlated traits listed under bright. For an illustration of writing showing a very keen thinker, refer to the bottom specimen shown under "comprehension."

BROAD-MINDED *ep* Tolerant of other people's opinions and behavior. This is revealed primarily in well-rounded circle formations as in *e, o, a,* and *g.* It may be found in both cool, poised, and warm, emotional natures.

Specimen 4

33

BROODY *e* The type of person who broods over things will reveal deep emotions, inhibitions, secrecy, and pessimism in his writing.

BROWBEATING *e* Intimidating with harsh words. When handwriting indicates that this is applicable to a person, it will show irritability, the tendency to domineer, sarcasm, and frankness.

BRUSQUE *e* Refer to the synonym, blunt.

BUNKER, M. N. The founder of Graphoanalysis, born July 4, 1892; died April 3, 1961. After many years of research, motivated by his own unquenchable thirst for greater understanding of human beings, he devoted the rest of his life to the sharing and dissemination of the knowledge he gained by empirical methods of observation.

BUOYANT *ep* One who has lightness of spirit and is cheerful can be considered optimistic. This is primarily shown in writing that slants upward (see Specimen 5). Other indications of the trait are found in upward-slanting *t* crossings and word finals.

Specimen 5

BUSYBODY *e* The writing of an inquisitive meddler, a gossip, will reveal over-talkativeness, an inquisitive mind, and frequently a highly developed imagination and love of

34

variety. Over-talkativeness is determined by an abundance of open-mouthed circle letters (see Specimen 6); an inquisitive mind is indicated by pointed *m's, n's, r's,* etc. The active imagination and love of variety are found in lower loops of *g, y,* and *j*; the wider and longer the loop, the greater is the imagination and love of variety.

Specimen 6

C

CAGEY *e* The sly, tricky, cunning individual reveals in his writing much deceit plus a certain amount of comprehension and analytical ability. There will be indications of shallow thinking, lack of intention to do one's best, doing just enough to fulfill one's own petty desires. The deceit is evident in double-looped circle letter formations; comprehension is shown in sharp points on *m, n, h,* and *r*; analytical ability in *y* strokes at the base line; shallow thinking appears in basin-like *t* crossings and shallow points on *m's, n's,* etc.

CALCULATING *e* One connotation of this adjective is very similar to that of cagey in that it means scheming or cunning. The other meanings, shrewd or cautious, may be applied when the writing shows strong analytical ability and a judicious nature and/or caution. Long finals or dashes used to fill in space at the right hand margin of a line of writing indicate caution.

CALLOUS (ED) *e* The unfeeling, insensitive writer writes with a perpendicular or backward slant, showing no sympathetic emotional responsiveness to others. There will be an absence of generosity and diplomacy.

CALM *e* The calm person is not high strung or highly expressive of emotions; he is neither irritable nor bellicose. As Specimen 1 illustrates, the slant will not show the variations of the emotionally immature nor the extreme slant to the right of the intensely emotional writer. The *i* and *j* dots will be either well-rounded (with no jabs) or circle dots.

this day is all

Specimen 1

CANDID *ep* The honest, outspoken individual is frank and aboveboard. This is primarily determined in the circle formations. The *a's, o's,* and *g's* (see Specimen 2) will either be open at the top or simply closed without either initial or final loops in them. The candid person will frequently show loyalty and a lack of bias.

an open mind
an open heart

Specimen 2

36

CANDOR *ep* This noun is an attribute that can be applied to the writer who has exactly the same characteristics as described above in candid: honesty, impartiality and frankness will be evident in the writing.

CANNY *e* Cautious: thrifty; shrewd. Caution is determined by long finals or dashes that fill out a line of writing; thriftiness is shown in conservative, narrow spacing of the writing with no generous, long finals to words (except at the end of the line); shrewdness is indicated by a combination of investigative and analytical strokes.

CAPABLE, CAPABILITY *e* Refer to able, ability.

CAPRICIOUS *e* The changeable, unpredictable person writes with a variable slant; his emotional reaction pattern is not stable. This will frequently be accompanied by long lower loops on *j*, *g*, and *y*, showing too many interests and much love of variety.

CAPTIOUS *e* When one is quick to find fault he will have analytical ability coupled with irritability, determined by sharp *v* strokes at the base line and jabs of the pen for *i* and *j* dots. There may be vanity and resentment present.

CAREFUL *e* This implies an element of caution, so there will likely be strokes in the writing indicating caution. There will be no highly emotional responsiveness. There will be close attention to detail (careful dotting of *i*'s and *j*'s near the points) and pride, as the careful person will take pride in doing a good job. Conservatism will be present.

CARELESS *e* This is an antonym of careful, so the opposite elements will be found in the handwriting. It will show no close attention to detail, but there will be impulsiveness, emotional responsiveness, and lack of a good sense of values.

CARNAL *e* The sensual, sexual individual is primarily interested in gratification of basic physical appetites. This is shown in heavy blotting of letters, filling in of what is ordinarily a loop or circle, and excessive corrugations in strokes. There will be an absence of the visionary or of the spiritual as revealed in large upper loops.

Reproduction of Specimen 3 may not reveal the corrugations that were evident in the original writing.

Specimen 3

CARPING *e* Refer to captious.

CASE HISTORY . One method of personality assessment that has been widely used by psychologists is the case history. All information possible about an individual or a group is collected and studied. This device can be of great value to Graphoanalysts who are working to produce further research data on Graphoanalysis and to those who specialize in counseling services.

CASTIGATION *e* Severe punishment, criticism, or rebuke can be directed either toward others or toward oneself. In the case of the former, the writing will have heavy, arrow-like *t* crossings (heavy sarcasm). They will often fall to the right of the *t* stem, showing high irritability or temper, and may slant downward to reveal the desire to domineer. In case of self-castigation, the strokes are whipped back to the left, showing the writer's desire to punish himself.

CASUAL *e* The nonchalant, indifferent writer has a cool, poised nature, lacking warmth and enthusiasm. The slant will be nearly vertical or completely vertical (see Specimen 4), the strokes will be light, and *t* crossings will be short.

Specimen 4

CAUSTIC *p* Sarcastic. This is determined by *t* crossings that come to a point at the end of the stroke. How light or how biting the sarcasm is (see Specimen 5) depends upon how light or how heavy the stroke is.

Specimen 5

CAUTION, CAUTIOUS *p* The prudent, circumspect writer is wary of taking chances. Caution is revealed (see Specimen 6) by long finals at the end of the line of writing.

CAVILER *e* One who resorts to trivial fault-finding will have some degree of analytical ability, but it will not be as pronounced as that of the captious individual. Other traits likely to be present are irritability, resentment, and pride.

CENSORIOUS *e* Inclined to find fault: critical. This type of person will have an analytical mind (*v* formations at the base line), frequently accompanied by such negative traits as irritability, sarcasm, resentment of imposition, and talkativeness.

CERTAIN *p* The sure, positive person reveals this attitude by making blunt final strokes in his writing. This is the opposite of the uncertainty shown in finals that taper to a weak point.

   Note the heavier pressure of the pen on the final strokes in Specimen 7. It is the writing of a man who always had the attitude that he knew he was right.

Specimen 7

40

CHANCE. A term used in Graphoanalytical and psychological statistical research work to compare actual or observed frequencies or percentages with those that could be expected on the basis of probability.

CHANGEABLE *ep* This is primarily determined when the slant of the writing varies a great deal. It is supported when the final strokes are weak (see Specimen 8), showing uncertainty.

Specimen 8

CHARACTER. In Graphoanalysis this term refers to an individual's pattern of behavior or personality, or his nature.

CHARACTERISTIC. This is used to designate a distinguishing trait of an individual.

CHARITABLE *e* This includes both kindness and generosity. There will be not only long finals and wide spacing between letters indicating a generous nature, but also a lack of harsh qualities.

CHARLATAN. Any person who pretends to knowledge of Graphoanalysis and to have the ability to use it without having either aptitude is an imposter. Reading a book or books about Graphoanalysis is not sufficient training to make one a competent Graphoanalyst.

CHARY *ep* Cautious: shy: frugal. All of these definitions denote a lack of giving of one's self or of one's possessions. Long finals at the end of a line, retraced formations, compression of the writing, lack of generous finals to words, and often self-consciousness (shown when the last stroke of *m* and *n* is higher than the rest of the letter) will be noticeable in the writing.

CHEERFUL *e* One condition of the extremely emotional nature. When one is filled with hope, he may be said to be optimistic; this is indicated by the upward slant of the line of writing, of words, or of strokes at the end of words. The tendency to optimism is also indicated when *t* crossings slant upward.

The girl who wrote Specimen 9 was popular with both students and teachers because of her cheerful disposition. She always looked on the bright side of things.

Specimen 9

CHILDISH *e* Immature. Evidence of this quality can be found in the writing of chronologically mature people who have not developed fully mentally and/or emotionally.

Such writing is characterized by weak formations, lack of strokes showing mental ability, decisiveness, will power, and other positive traits.

CHOLERIC *ep* The writer who is quick-tempered or easily angered will show either of these conditions in heavy jabs for *i* and *j* dots, or by short inflexible tick strokes, or in *t* bars placed to the right of the *t* stem—or in combinations of these strokes.

CHOOSY *p* This adjective may be used in relation to choice of close personal friends when the writer is particular or selective in this respect. It is shown in Specimen 10 by narrow lower loops in *g, y,* or *j*.

Specimen 10

CIRCUMSPECT *e* Refer to careful and cautious. The writing of a circumspect person will have the nearly vertical slant showing cool judgment. There will likely be retraced *t* and *d* stems showing dignity; closely dotted *i's* and *j's* showing attention to details; long finals at the end of the line showing caution.

CLAIRVOYANT *e* A person who has clairvoyance (keen perception or great insight) reveals this in needle points in *m's, n's,* etc., accompanied by the frequent breaks in the body of words that show intuition.

43

CLANNISH *p* Tending to associate closely, to the exclusion of others. This indicates a very high degree of selectivity, to the point of exclusiveness, and is determined by small squares or round circles (see Specimen 11) in place of loops on *g, y,* and *j.*

Specimen 11

CLEVER *ep* This means bright, quick-witted, and will be revealed in sharply pointed *m's, n's, h's* and *r's.* It can often be applied to the writer who shows a combination of good sense of humor and light sarcasm.

CLINICAL. This is one method that was widely used by M. N. Bunker in determining and proving basic stroke values in Graphoanalysis. It is based on actual treatment and observation of subjects, as distinguished from experimental or laboratory study.

CLOD *e* A dull, stupid individual shows no indications in his writing of comprehension or of analytical ability.

CLOSE-LIPPED, CLOSE-MOUTHED *p* These adjectives refer to people who talk little; they are reticent. This characteristic is shown in the circle letters (see Specimen 12) when they are closed with a tie stroke, never left open.

44

collection for biology cla

Specimen 12

COARSE *e* Lacking refinement. There will be an absence of cultural or considerate traits in the writing, with a likely show of ostentation and sensuality.

COCKSURE *e* Sure or self-confident to an offensive degree. Any positive trait, when present to an extreme degree, can become a liability rather than an asset. The writing of a cocksure person will show an excessive amount of underscoring in his writing and signature, and/or extremely blunt final strokes.

COCKY *e* This is determined by a combination of conceit and self-confidence. The *t* and *d* stems will be very high and the signature and/or other words will frequently be underscored.

COLD *ep* Without warmth of feeling: without enthusiasm. Lack of emotional responsiveness and sympathy are shown in the vertical or backward slant; lack of enthusiasm is shown in very short strokes for *t* crossings.

COLD-HEARTED *ep* The writing of the unsympathetic, unfeeling, unkind person will not only be vertical or backward in slant, but will show a lack of generosity and depth of feeling.

COLLECTED *p* The calm, poised individual may have a sympathetic nature, but will not show high emotional reactions. Organizational ability, determined by an equal

45

balance of loops above and below the line (see Specimen 13), is often found in the writing of one who uses cool judgment as opposed to emotional feelings in reaching decisions.

far from

Specimen 13

COMMON-SENSE *e* Having practical judgment is applicable to the writer whose *t* crossings are not placed above the *t* stems, who has a good sense of values or is conservative, and whose lower loops are more predominant than his upper loops. Larger lower loops show a more active imagination in practical than in theoretical fields.

Specimen 14 is the writing of a housewife who, in spite of her husband's impracticality, always managed to keep the family going on a common-sense basis.

turn an ordinary day in

free to enjoy little thing

Specimen 14

46

COMPANIONABLE *e* The sociable, friendly person has a sympathetic nature, is not exclusive or clannish, is tolerant and broad-minded, and is not deceitful.

COMPASSIONATE *e* One who feels and shows deep sympathy for others writes with a forward slant and with a broad, heavy stroke. Generosity and frankness are usually present.

COMPATIBLE, COMPATIBILITY *e* To determine whether or not two people are capable of getting along well together, one must first Graphoanalyze the handwriting of each individual. Then, by a simple reasoning process, one can decide from the similarities and dissimilarities shown whether or not the two can work or live together harmoniously.

COMPENSATION. In psychology, this is called a defense mechanism whereby one attempts to disguise an undesired trait by exaggerating a desired or socially approved one.

COMPLACENT *e* One who is self-satisfied or smug shows a combination of vanity and narrow-mindedness in his writing.

COMPLAISANT *e* This involves a willingness to please, an obliging and agreeable nature. Such a person is revealed when the writing shows a sympathetic or responsive nature, some yielding strokes, a desire to conform, generosity, and a lack of resentment, irritability and positiveness.

COMPLIANT *ep* The yielding, submissive person shows yielding strokes in his writing. Such strokes are particularly noticeable in the sprawling, rounded, unformed

47

s. The writing will lack indications of strong will power, decisiveness, and determination.

COMPOSED *p* Calm, self-possessed, cool. This is shown in a near-vertical or vertical slant.

Specimen 15, written by a high school coach, shows that the writer had some irritability (note the *i* dots). This, however, he did not reveal to the public (note the vertical slant). His composure was marked.

Specimen 15

COMPREHENSION *p* The ability to understand, to grasp ideas. This is indicated by sharp points, as in *m, n, r,* etc. The degree of the writer's comprehension (see Specimen 16) is determined by the length of the needle-point strokes.

a

Specimen 16

48

b

c

COMPREHENSIVE *p* Understanding much. See "comprehension" above.

CONCEITED *p* One who has an exaggerated opinion of himself is considered vain. This trait is revealed in exceedingly tall *t* and *d* stems.

The young man who wrote Specimen 17 was married briefly to three different girls during his four years in college. His conceit was no asset when it came to marital adjustment.

Specimen 17

CONCENTRATION *p* Close or fixed attention. The writer who is able to center his attention on one thing to the exclusion of other stimuli reveals this ability in small writing. Loops do not extend into lines above and below the line of writing. By observing and comparing many specimens of writing, the Graphoanalyst can judge this quantitatively, i.e., he can determine the degree to which a writer possesses this ability (see Specimen 18). When present to a marked degree, concentration affects every other trait shown in the writing; for example, when temper is evident along with concentration, the expression of temper will be greater because of the force of the concentration.

Specimen 18

CONFORMITY *p* Action in accordance with rules, customs, etc. The desire to conform to socially acceptable standards of conduct is shown in tall, retraced *t* and *d* stems.

Specimen 19

CONFUSED *e* A mixed up person will show disorder and confusion in his handwriting. This is often evident in a slant that varies from one extreme to the other and in large loops that extend into the writing on lines above and below the line of writing.

CONJECTURE. Guesswork has no part in Graphoanalysis. Graphoanalyses must be based on observable evidence and logical conclusions deduced from that evidence.

CONSCIENTIOUS *e* The honest individual who acts in accordance with what he knows is right will show loyalty to his ideals (small, round dots over *i* and *j*) and frankness, lack of deceit. Persistence often accompanies this trait.

CONSERVATIVE *ep* A conservative person tends to keep his energy and his belongings from being lost or wasted. This is determined from the writing when it is compressed (see Specimen 20), when there are no long spaces between letter formations, and when stem formations are retraced.

Specimen 20

CONSIDERATE *e* Having or showing regard for others and their feelings. The slant of such a writer will be forward enough to show a sympathetic nature. Broadmindedness will be evident, with a lack of negative traits such as vanity, resentment, and a desire to domineer.

51

CONSPICUOUS *ep* People who attract attention by being unusual or outstanding usually have large writing with well-made flourishes and unusually large, well-formed signatures.

CONSTRAINT *ep* Repression of natural feelings or behavior shows in compressed or cramped strokes. Refer to "repressed".

CONTENTIOUS *e* See "argumentative".

CONTRADICTORY. Traits that are contrary to or inconsistent with each other often appear in handwriting. For example, one person's writing may show both talkativeness and secretiveness, or strong will power and weak will power. Not only must evaluation be used, but the Graphoanalyst must also learn to use quantitative as well as qualitative judgment. Some individuals are more consistent than others, but no human being is completely consistent in his behavior.

CONVENTIONAL *p* Conforming to formal or accepted standards; refer to conformity.

COOL *e* A calm, dispassionate emotional nature is revealed in light line writing that has a near-vertical slant.

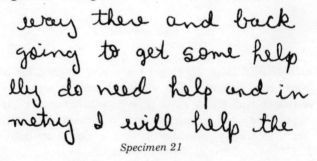

Specimen 21

52

COQUETTISH *ep* See "flirtatious".

COURAGEOUS *e* A brave person will show in his writing such positive traits as self-reliance and definiteness, with a lack of timidity and repression. Impulsiveness is sometimes taken for courage, but real courage involves the actual facing and dealing with something dangerous, difficult, or painful, instead of withdrawing from it.

CRAFTY *e* Subtly deceitful. Refer to "artful".

CREATIVE *ep* One who is able to create, to make, to construct with the hands, reveals this ability by making broad, rounded or flat-topped *m's, n's* and *r's* (see Specimen 22). Other types of creative ability may be revealed when there is a combination of analytical ability, keen comprehension, and artistic, musical, or literary ability.

Specimen 22

CREDULOUS *e* The person who is inclined to believe too readily, who is easily convinced, is revealed when there is an absence of investigative and analytical strokes in his writing. The upper loops, showing philosophical, religious, or theoretical thinking, will be rounded, not pointed, at the top. Such a writer has no desire to investigate or explore ideas for himself, but simply believes what he is told or what he reads.

CRITICAL *ep* Tending to find fault: characterized by careful analysis. Analytical ability, shown in *v*-formations at the base line (see Specimen 23), will be prominent in the writing of a critical individual, and is usually combined with sarcasm, resentment, and an investigative mind.

Specimen 23

CROSS *ep* An ill-tempered, easily annoyed writer shows this trait in jabbed *i* and *j* dots and/or *t* crossings made to the right of the *t* stem, or short tick strokes at the beginning of a group of strokes.

CULTURED *ep* The desire for culture (refinement) is determined primarily by Greek *e's* and figure-eight *g's* as shown in Specimen 24, but can also be determined by combinations of one or both of these with other traits.

Specimen 24

CUNNING *e* Although one meaning of this is simply skillful; clever; shrewd: it also has a connotation of skillful in deception. In either case determination of the trait will be based on keen analytical thinking; in the latter case it will involve deceit or secretiveness, lack of frankness.

CUPIDITY *ep* Strong desire, especially for wealth; greed. Hooks at the beginning of stroke formations show a desire to acquire; when such initial hooks are predominant in the writing, and when the writing is heavy with no long finals to indicate generosity, the writer may be considered to possess cupidity.

CURIOUS *p* Inquisitive. A writer reveals his desire to learn when he makes his *m's, n's, r's,* etc., with inverted *v* formations.

The student who wrote Specimen 25 was the type who was never satisfied to find out only facts required by the professor; he was always prying into many different fields of knowledge. Notice how often the inverted *v* formation appears in this small sample of his writing.

Specimen 25

CUTTING *ep* Wounding the feelings. Refer to sarcastic.

CYNICAL *ep* Although this is a synonym of pessimistic, besides the downward slant of words or lines of writing, there will often also be indications of sarcasm (*t* bars that come to arrow-like points).

D

DABBLER *e* One who does something superficially, not seriously, will show in his writing a combination of a love of change and variety (large lower loops on *g*, *y*, and *j*) and shallowness (basin-like *t* crossings). The investigative inclination will likely be revealed, but the points on the *m's* and *n's* will be shallow rather than deep penetrating points.

DAFT *e* The writing of a weak-minded person will be lacking in such positive qualities as comprehension, will power, decisiveness, a good sense of values, determination and persistence.

DANGEROUS *e* This term is a broad one and must be used with great care. An individual who is likely to cause injury or pain, either to himself or to others, may be considered dangerous. The writer who shows great depth of feeling (very heavy, broad lines) plus repression of feelings (narrow, retraced, squeezed writing), but who lacks the ability to express his emotions, is one who is likely to suffer an explosive emotional outburst when pressures upon him become too great. Such an outburst may cause actual physical injury. One might also consider dangerous the writer who reveals a lack of honesty, who is deceitful to a high degree and who is overly acquisitive at the same time. This type of person may well cause injury by taking for himself that which belongs to another. The term could be applied equally fittingly to one who is very frank and outspoken and at the same time is extremely sarcastic.

DARING *e* The fearless, bold person shows in his writing initiative and/or aggressiveness; there will be strong, forward-swinging strokes in *p, g,* and *y*. His self-reliance will be revealed by strong underscores. He will likely show definiteness of thinking in strong or blunt final strokes, keenness of thinking in sharp-pointed *m's* and *n's*, and independence of thinking and acting in short *d* and *t* stems.

DASHING *e* This carries a connotation of boldness plus liveliness and sometimes means showy. Such a writer will have a combination of enthusiasm, emotional responsiveness, initiative, comprehension, and in the case of the second interpretation, there will be unnecessary flourishes indicating ostentation.

DASTARDLY *e* One who is both cowardly and mean is a weak individual who will show in his writing a lack of self-reliance, initiative, independence, and determination. At the same time he may reveal sarcasm, the desire to domineer, temper, or sensuality.

DAUNTLESS *e* Refer to "brave".

DAYDREAMER *p* The unrealistic, visionary planner or schemer reveals this bent of mind by placing his *t* bars above the *t* stem. The bars will be light, but they may be long if the individual feels enthusiastic about his daydreams.

The young woman who wrote Specimen 1 had a certain amount of enthusiasm when she first planned a project, but that enthusiasm did not last very long. In a short while she forgot about the original plan and started daydreaming about something entirely different.

57

The people there, their anxious to see them

Specimen 1

DEAD PAN *p* Poker face. These slang expressions refer to a person who assumes a complete lack of expression on his face. The ability to do this is revealed in circle letters such as *a, o,* and *g* when they are completely closed with a final loop formation that is approximately as large as the circle letter itself.

The *o's* in *born, loved, love* and *our* in Specimen 2 are excellent illustrations of this faculty.

born helpless, and so must be the love- our

Specimen 2

DEBAUCHED *e* Extremely indulgent of one's appetites, especially for sensual pleasure. Such a writer will have heavy writing, heavily blotted and corrugated, with a lack of such positive character traits as self-control, pride and dignity.

DEBONAIR *e* One interpretation of this is the same as affable. When using the connotation gay, look for evidence of optimism in addition to the qualities found in an affable writer. This is shown in the upward slant of the writing itself or of *t* crossings and word endings.

58

DECEIT *p* Making one believe what is not true; deluding; misleading; lying. Self-deceit is determined when a circle letter formation has an initial loop within the letter; double loops (both initial and final loop, shown also in Specimen 3) in the small circle letters indicate intentional deceit.

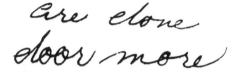

Specimen 3

DECEITFUL, DECEIVING, DECEPTIVE   *p* Tending to deceit or deceive. See above.

DECENT *ep* The person who wants to conform to approved social standards reveals this desire in tall, retraced *d* and *t* stems, which also indicate pride and dignity. Whether or not the writer will conform to such standards must be evaluated, however, from the relative strength of this trait compared with others present in the writing that either add to or detract from the evidence.

The woman who wrote Specimen 4 was considered by others to be very proper and respectable. In addition to pride and dignity, her writing shows reserve, kindliness without exaggeration, and rhythm; there is a lack of sensuality and dishonesty.

Specimen 4

59

DECIDED, DECISIVE *p* These adjectives can mean either definite or determined. Refer to their explanations.

DECOROUS *e* Characterized by showing propriety and good taste. This is a synonym of decent (see above) but implies more stiffness and formality in observance of standards of conduct, so the writing will be more precise.

DECREPIT *e* Shaky, corrugated, wavering strokes reveal one who is worn out either by old age or illness.

DEDUCTION. The process of reaching a conclusion by reasoning from the general to the specific is important to proper assessment of personality through Graphoanalysis. It is the untrained or unskilled Graphoanalyst who expresses himself in such generalities that a Graphoanalysis might apply equally well to many individuals.

DEFENSE MECHANISMS. In psychological terminology these terms are adjustive processes used by both normal and abnormal persons to justify or vindicate their actions in order to maintain their self-respect, prestige and sense of security. They may forget reality by indulging in phantasy or daydreaming; they may distort reality by the use of rationalizing or giving plausible reasons for inconsistent and undesirable behavior; they may atone for reality by compensating for some personal deficiency through achieving success in and excelling in another line of endeavor, by feigning illness or physical disability, or by regressing to a childish level of living; or they may retreat from reality through functional dissociation.

An understanding of these defense mechanisms and how they are used in important to a Graphoanalyst. Such knowledge can give the Graphoanalyst an insight as to why some individuals disclaim possessing certain personality traits that are quite evident in their handwriting, even when other personality tests reveal the same characteristics.

DEFIANT *e* One who openly and boldly resists authority or opposition will show in his writing independence of thought and action, resentment, initiative or aggression, frankness, and stubbornness.

DEFINITE *p* The certain, positive person illustrated in Specimen 5 writes with blunt final stroke endings.

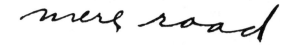

Specimen 5

DELIBERATE *p* Careful in considering; slow, unhurried. This is determined by separated stems in *d* and *t* (see Specimen 6) and is usually accompanied by the well-rounded *m's* and *n's* that indicate the logical type of mind.

men don't

Specimen 6

DELUDING, DELUSIVE *p* Refer to deceitful and deceit.

DEMOCRATIC *e* One who considers and treats others as one's equals, who is not snobbish, shows broadmindedness and tolerance in his writing. There will be no indi-

61

cations of vanity or the desire to domineer.

DEMONSTRATIVE *ep* Showing feelings openly and frankly. The greater the degree of slant to the right the writing has on the emotional gauge, the more likely is the writer to show his feelings. He will express them vocally when this slant is accompanied by open-mouthed or wide circle formations (as in *a, o,* and *g*). Signs of timidity, secretiveness, deceit, or other inhibiting qualities will decrease the extent to which the writer is demonstrative.

DENSE *e* A thick-headed or stupid person shows no indications in his writing of comprehension; his strokes reveal an extremely slow thinker.

DEPENDABLE *e* To determine whether or not a person is trustworthy and reliable, there should be evidences in his writing of honesty, pride, persistence, determination, and other positive characteristics. There should be a lack of deceit, emotional immaturity, indecisiveness, and other negative traits.

DEPENDENT *e* One who is influenced or controlled by someone else will reveal yielding strokes such as the sprawled, unformed *s*; he will usually have weak will power and indecisiveness (final strokes grow lighter at the end).

The Student who wrote Specimen 7 depended on the professor to tell her what to read and what to do; she depended on parents and friends in the same manner; she was easily influenced by others. Note the sprawled *s's* and weak finals. In almost every instance in the complete specimen the *t* crossings became lighter at the end, indicating will power that weakens if opposition is encountered.

62

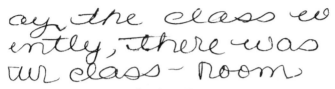

Specimen 7

DEPRAVED *e* Morally bad; corrupt; perverted. Marked sensuality will be the most prominent evidence in the writing. Heavy lines with frequent blurs and blottings and corrugations of the lines reveal preoccupation with and over-indulgence in sensual pleasures. There will be a lack of positive character traits such as frankness, generosity, etc.

DEPRESSION *e* This is an emotional condition that is experienced by most normal people; it is pathological when it is severe enough to interfere with the individual's adjustment to everyday living. Intensely emotionally expressive writers experience this phase more often and to a greater degree than do those who have less expressive natures. It also occurs more frequently to pessimistic than to optimistic writers.

DEPTH OF EMOTIONS *p* The extent to which an individual absorbs emotional experiences, the strength and endurance of the emotions he feels, is determined by the width or heaviness of his written strokes. The light line writer experiences the same emotions that a heavy line writer does, but they do not affect him for as long a period of time.

Because of the prevalence of the use of ball point pens, one must exercise great care in judging the depth of a person's writing. A thorough study of Graphoanalysis is necessary to become expert in this or any other facet of handwriting analysis.

63

DERANGED *e* Marked disorder of the mind appears as marked disorder in the handwriting. When such writing is observed, referral to a competent authority in mental disorders is imperative.

DESPONDENT *e* Any extremely emotionally reactive person experiences this state of feeling at times. It is increased when evidence of pessimism is present, when the line of writing, words, or finals of words have a downward slant.

DESPOTIC *p* Refer to domineering.

DETACHED *p* The aloof person, not involved in emotional interest in others, reveals this trait in his vertical or backhand slant. Quite often clannishness is present.

Note the small, squared, lower circle loops in Specimen 8. It was written by a young woman who was considered a "snob" by her peer group.

yesterday my dad didnt
sister didnt have to go to scl
a holiday. They teased me a
because I accomplished som

Specimen 8

DETERMINATION *p* The quality of being resolute; firmness of purpose. This is revealed in heavy downstrokes written below the base line of writing. The strength of the determination is judged by the width or heaviness of the stroke compared to the rest of the writing; the endurance of the determination is indicated by the relative

64

length of the downstroke.

Although Specimen 9 shows the single stroke below the *y* rather than a loop, the downstroke of loops on *y, g,* and *j* may be judged in the same manner.

Specimen 9

DETERMINED *ep* Resolved: unwavering. See "determination" above.

DETRIMENTAL. Personality traits which may prove harmful to the writer or to others are considered detrimental if they are observed in the writing. Although this is generally applied to those traits that are considered negative, even positive traits can be detrimental when present to such a degree that the writer lacks balance.

DEVOUT *e* This implies sincere devotion to one's faith and is evidenced in large upper loops showing a philosophical or spiritual bent of mind, and small, round *i* and *j* dots showing loyalty to or faith in one's ideals.

DEXTERITY, DEXTEROUS *e* These are applicable to either physical or mental skill. For physical dexterity, look for the well rounded *m's* and *n's* and square topped *r's* accompanied by a good sense of rhythm. Desire for physical activity may be present. Mental dexterity, or cleverness, is revealed in the sharp comprehension points on *m's, n's,* and *h's* plus fluidity of thought, figure-eight *g's*. Analytical ability and a sense of humor are often in evidence.

DICTATORIAL *p* This implies the domineering, autocratic methods or manner of a dictator. Refer to domineering.

DIFFERENT *p* The desire to be different, to be unlike most others, is determined in small circles used over *i* and *j* instead of a dot.

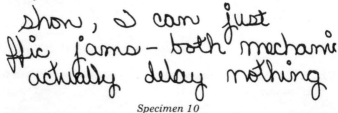

Specimen 10

DIFFIDENT *e* Hesitant to assert oneself; shy. This may be evident from retraced and even compressed *m's, n's* and other letters, showing conservatism or timidity. It is especially pronounced when self-consciousness is present—when the last stroke of the *m* and *n* is higher than the rest of the letter.

The man who wrote Specimen 11 was so diffident, so shy and self-conscious, that it was torment to him to have to speak out in a group of people. Notice the hump on the last stroke of the *m's* and *n's*.

Specimen 11

DIGNIFIED *ep* One who has a lofty manner, stateliness, or calm self-possession does not write with a high degree of emotional slant. *T* and *d* stems are retraced and high in proportion to the body of the writing. The script will usually be carefully and precisely written.

Specimen 12 was written by a public school teacher who was noted for his calm, dignified manner of conducting his classrooms.

When these were presented without the omissions.

Specimen 12

DILETTANTE *e* One who follows an art or science for amusement only and in a superficial way will show similar characteristics to the "dabbler". This noun is the more applicable of the two when, in addition to traits specified under "dabbler", there is evidence of a desire for culture. This is shown in the Greek *e* and figure-eight *g*.

DILIGENT *e* Persevering and careful in work. This is determined when there are frequent tie loops in the writing (persistence) combined with careful dotting of the *i* and *j* (attention to detail). Strong will power and determination lend supporting evidence.

Specimen 13 was taken from the writing of a student who, though not the fastest thinker in the class, made top marks because of her persistence in applying herself and her careful attention to details.

embroideries from Bulg with intricate designs

Specimen 13

DIPLOMATIC *p* One who is tactful and adroit in dealing with people shows this ability in writing that tapers at the finish of words without losing the identity of the strokes. It is also evident in stroke groups such as those of *m* and *n* (see Specimen 14) when the last stroke is noticeably smaller than the first.

Specimen 14

DISAGREEABLE *e* Hard to get along with. This is determined when such negative traits as the following are prominent in the writing: resentment, vanity, desire to domineer, self-interest, irritability, temper, over-sensitiveness to criticism, or bluntness and frankness without tact.

DISCERNMENT *p* Keen perception or judgment. Refer to "comprehension".

DISCREET *p* The writer who is careful about what he says and does reveals this by filling in spaces at the end of lines of writing with long final strokes. See "cautious".

Specimen 15

DISCRIMINATING *e* Able to make or see fine distinctions. This is determined when the writing shows comprehension and analytical ability (see Specimen 15). The slant is likely to be near-vertical, vertical, or backhand, as emotional responsiveness interferes with judgment.

DISDAINFUL *e* When a writer regards others as beneath his dignity or status, when he is scornful and aloof, his *d* and *t* stems will be retraced and very high, showing pride and dignity, and his slant will be vertical or near-vertical, showing a cool, aloof nature.

DISHONEST *p* See "deceitful", "deceit".

DISINGENUOUS *ep* Not straightforward; insincere. Determined when there is intentional deceit and shallowness in the writing.

DISPASSIONATE *e* The person who is free from passion, emotion or bias (see Specimen 16) writes with a vertical or near-vertical slant (cool nature) and with a light pressure of the pen (light depth of emotions).

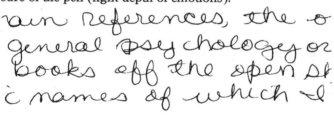

Specimen 16

DISQUIETUDE *ep* Restlessness is revealed by large upper or lower loops that interfere with the script on the line above or below the line of writing; also by variable slant, with some strokes slanting forward and some backward.

DISSEMBLE *e* One who conceals his true feelings and motives by pretense shows in his writing intentional de-

69

ceit, inhibitions, and diplomatic ability to the point of hypocrisy.

DISSENTIOUS *e* Quarrelsome. Look for strokes showing resentment, irritability, talkativeness, analytical ability, tendency to domineer, and self-interest.

DISSIPATED *e* Indulging in pleasure to excess. The writing of such an individual will be marked by sensuality and absence of self-control.

DISTANT *p* Cool in manner; aloof. This is basically due to the emotional nature of the individual, and is determined (as shown in Specimen 17) when the writing has a vertical or backhand slant.

Specimen 17

DISTRAIT *e* Refer to absent-minded.

DISTRAUGHT *e* A mentally confused person is revealed in sprawling script or in any disordered writing with variable slant.

Specimen 18 is an outstanding example of the writing of a very confused young man.

Specimen 18

DISTURBED *e* Unsettled normal mental calm or powers of concentration. See "distraught" above.

DOCILE *e* Easy to discipline; tractable. Look for frequent yielding strokes and lack of strong will power, determination, and stubbornness.

DOGMATIC *e* A dogmatic individual states his opinions in a positive or arrogant manner whether or not they have a factual basis. His writing will show the blunt final strokes of positiveness, possibly accompanied by narrow-mindedness and conservatism.

DOMINATING *p* Ruling or controlling by superior power. Such a person reveals this ability in his *t* crossings (see Specimen 19): they are very heavy, broad, in relation to the rest of the writing, showing a forceful will power.

The time to

Specimen 19

DOMINANT. Those personality characteristics that appear most pronouncedly and frequently in the handwriting of an individual are considered to be his dominant traits. This is in contrast with traits that are merely indicated, but not evident to any great degree. Such traits are thought of an minor traits.

DOMINEERING *p* The tyrannical, overbearing, arrogant person, Specimen 20, reveals this characteristic in arrow-like *t* bars that are slanted downward.

Don't do it

Specimen 20

DOODLES Marks made in aimless scribbling can be evalu-

ated for purposes of determining personality characteristics. This, however, can be done only through study
of the Advanced Course in Graphoanalysis. It entails
too much detail of observation to be described here.

DOTAGE *e* A feeble and childish state due to old age.
See "senility".

DOUBLE-FACED *e* Hypocritical, insincere people show
intentional deceit (double-looped circle letters) and diplomacy (tapering of words or stroke combinations) to a
high degree. Although diplomatic ability can be a decided asset (even deceit can be under certain circumstances),
when it is prominent in the writing and is accompanied
by deceit, one can well doubt the sincerity of the writer.

DRAMATIC *p* The highly emotional person shows how he
feels; he responds and reacts to others and to emotional
situations. This is determined when the slant of the writing
registers from *C* forward on the emotional gauge.

The writer of Specimen 21 found an outlet for his emo-
tionality by being a frequent participant in community
theater plays. His love of the dramatic is enhanced by
his desire to culture, which is evidenced by the *r's* that
are made like Greek *e's*.

Specimen 21

DREAMER *p* Refer to "daydreamer".

DRIVE *e* The force to go, to push forward, shows in the vigorous, forceful, forward strokes in writing. Mentally energetic and ambitious people write with a forceful hand that portrays their inner drive.

DRUNK, DRUNKEN Handwriting that is done under the influence of liquor or of an intoxicating, powerful emotion portrays the change in personality that is present, just as other expressive movements of the individual differ from those that are normally characteristic of him.

DULL *e* Writing of a mentally slow, stupid person shows an absence of strokes indicating comprehension or analytical ability.

DUPLICITY *ep* Hypocritical cunning or deception. Refer to "double-faced".

DYNAMIC *e* Energetic; vigorous; forceful. Such a person shows a forceful forward swing to his writing, with enthusiasm, will power, and lack of inhibitions or timidity.

E

EAGER *e* This implies great enthusiasm in the desire for something, so the writing of an eager person will reveal the desire to have, to get (shown in initial hooks), plus strong enthusiasm (long, heavy *t* crossings). If there are frequent inverted *v* formations, one can assume that the writer is eager to learn.

EARNEST *e* The serious and intense individual goes about doing something with determination. His writing will therefore show lack of deceit, strong determination (heavy downstrokes below the base line), loyalty to his ideals (small, round *i* and *j* dots), and an absence of ostentation.

EARTHY *e* Of this world, hence simple and natural; determined when lower loops are more predominant than upper loops in the writing (practical rather than theoretical imagination), when letters such as *b* that normally start with a loop are made with a single downstroke instead of a loop (simplicity and directness), and when there is a lack of deceit and ostentation.

EASY-GOING *e* The writer who deals with things in an unhurried, unworried manner shows deliberateness in his writing. Refer to "deliberate".

EBULLIENT *e* Overflowing with enthusiasm and high spirits. Such an individual writes with a forward slant; the degree of his ebullience is determined by how far forward the slant measures on the emotional gauge and how strong and long are his *t* crossings. The longer and heavier the *t* bars, the greater is his enthusiasm.

ECCENTRIC *p* The desire to be different from other people, to be unconventional in some way, is evident when a writer uses a small circle for a dot over *i* and *j* (see Specimen 1). The degree or type of eccentricity cannot be determined from this alone, but it is always a definite indication of some idiosyncracy.

74

Specimen 1

ECONOMICAL *ep* When a person is thrifty, his writing will have a compressed appearance. There will be narrow spaces between letters and words and a lack of long finals indicating extravagant generosity.

EFFEMINATE *e* Qualities such as weakness, gentleness, and delicacy are commonly attributed to women, so the writer who reveals such traits may be referred to as effeminate. This term must be used discreetly, however, as men usually consider such an allusion offensive.

EFFERVESCENT *e* A vivacious person writes with an energetic, forceful, forward sweep of the pen. The slant will be a forward one, there will be enthusiasm and talkativeness evident.

EFFICIENT *ep* Such a person writes with an absence of wasted motion. His writing frequently shows keen comprehension and creative ability.

EFFUSIVE *e* One who is too demonstrative, who expresses excessive emotion in an unrestrained manner, and will write with the far forward slant that shows the intensely emotionally expressive nature. There will be a lack of such inhibiting traits as caution, secrecy, and conservatism.

75

EGOCENTRIC *e* Viewing everything in relation to oneself. The writing of an egocentric slants from vertical to backhand, showing no sympathetic responsiveness toward others. There will be conservatism, narrow-mindedness, vanity, and a complete absence of generosity.

EGOISTIC (AL), EGOTISTIC (AL) *e* A conceited, selfish, self-centered individual shows in his writing exaggerated pride (to the point of vanity), lack of generosity, and often uses circles for *i* and *j* dots, and unnecessary flourishes, showing his individualism and ostentation.

ELOQUENT *e* Having speech or writing that is forceful, fluent, graceful, and persuasive. Fluidity of thought or speech is evident in graceful, flowing lines, as in *f*'s made with a smoothly inverted lower loop, or figure-eight *g* formations. Forcefulness and persuasiveness are shown in the energetic forward movement of the pen and strong final stroke endings.

EMBRYONIC This may be used to refer to a trait that is rudimentary but has not as yet been developed. Indications only of the trait will be evident in the writing; it will not be prominent.

EMOTIONAL *ep* Showing emotion—love, hate, fear, anger, etc.; easily aroused to emotion. This is primarily determined through use of the emotional gauge. The farther to the right the writing slants, the more emotional is the writer. Evaluation must be used to determine the extent to which restraining influences such as timidity, secrecy, caution, and self-consciousness will affect the writer's emotional expression. Refer to "foundation", "emotional".

76

EMPHATIC *p* The definite, forceful individual writes with a heavier pressure of the pen at the end of his strokes (see Specimen 2), giving them a blunt appearance.

Specimen 2

EMPIRICAL. Relying and based solely on experiment and observation; relying or based on practical experience. Graphoanalysis has been tested over a period of almost forty years by thousands of Graphoanalysts through the use of the empirical method.

ENERGETIC *e* This is determined when there is a vigorous, forceful, forward movement of the pen and frequently includes initiative and aggressiveness.

ENTERPRISING *e* Full of energy and initiative; ambitious. The former is shown when there is a forward swing of the pen in *p, g, j,* and *y*; the latter is applicable when this stroke is prominent and the *t's* are crossed well up on the stem, but not far enough to indicate mere daydreaming.

The enterprising young man who wrote Specimen 3 developed his own business of raising and selling unusual tropical fish while he was still a student. By the time he was out of school, he had moved the business from his home to a building where he had to employ an assistant to help him take care of the business. The stroke from the *t* to the top of the *h* in "that" indicates the same forceful forward sweep as do the *g* strokes.

Specimen 3

ENTHUSIASTIC *ep* The person who has or shows intense or ardent interest, and who is capable of arousing such interest or zeal in others, crosses his *t*'s with a sweeping stroke shown in Specimen 4. The force of his enthusiasm is determined by the weight of the *t* crossing in relation to the rest of the writing; the endurance of his enthusiasm is determined by the length of the stroke.

Specimen 4

ENVIOUS *e* Characterized by envy. This is based on a desire to acquire something possessed by someone else, accompanied by a feeling of jealousy. Acquisitiveness and jealousy will appear in the writing of an envious person. The former is determined by initial hooks, the latter by a small, squared initial loop. This loop is frequently apparent on *m's, n's,* and *w's,* especially capitals, but may be found at the beginning of many other letters.

Jealousy in Specimen 5 is indicated by the initial stroke of the capital *i's.* Acquisitiveness is evident in the frequent initial hooks.

Specimen 5

EQUABLE *e* One who has an equable temperament is steady and serene. His writing will show very little fluctuation, either in slant or other aspects. The slant may be backhand, vertical, or B-C. There will be no indications of irritability and temper.

EQUANIMITY *e* One who possesses equanimity is equable. See above.

EROTIC *ep* A person who is abnormally sensitive to sexual stimulation usually writes with heavy strokes, showing sensuousness, with some blots and corrugations, showing sensuality, and with a forward slant, showing that he is emotionally responsive.

EROTICISM *p* Preoccupation with sex. Refer to "sensual".

ERRATIC *e* One meaning of this adjective is deviating from the conventional or customary course. Refer to "eccentric".

Specimen 6 was written by a woman who rarely dressed in feminine clothes and who did not accept the sex role of a female. She always dotted her *i's* and *j's* with a circle. Her *t* bars were never *t* crossings; she made them come down through the top of her *t's*, which were either loops or hooks. Do not draw the conclusion from this that circle *i* dots indicate sexual abnormality; they merely indicate some idiosyncracy, and are pointed out because they add evidence to the erraticism of this particular writer.

Specimen 6

ERUPTIVE *e* The person who is likely to have a sudden outburst of emotion writes with a heavy stroke (deep emotions), a vertical slant (lack of emotional expressiveness), and cramped writing (repression). An individual with this combination of traits may go for a long period of time without revealing his true feelings because of repression and lack of ability to express himself. When tension mounts too high, however, he is likely to express his feelings in an explosive manner.

ESTHETE *e* See "aesthete".

ETHEREAL *e* Opposite of earthly. When a writer has this quality, high upper loops will be predominant in his writing. Such loops indicate imagination or thinking along spiritual or philosophical lines. There may be frequent breaks between the letters of a word, showing a psychic strain. The writing usually is light line; heavy writing indicates more interest in sensuous pleasures.

EVASIVE *e* Not straightforward. The writing of such a person will show cleverness, deceitfulness, diplomacy, and lack of simplicity and directness.

EVEN-TEMPERED *e* Refer to "calm".

EXCITABLE *e* One who is easily aroused emotionally writes with a far forward slant and the writing frequently shows irritability, temper or resentment.

EXCLUSIVE *p* Refer to "clannish".

EXHIBITIONIST *e* The person who likes to call attention to himself, to show off, often makes his capital letters quite large in proportion to the lower case letters and uses superfluous flourishes in his writing.

EXPANSIVE *e* An expansive person is generous, sympathetic, and demonstrative. His writing will show generosity in long finals on words and wide spaces between letter combinations, a slant indicating emotional responsiveness, and frankness and broadmindedness.

EXPLORATORY *p* Investigative. One who likes to learn new things and who has the ability to learn shows this in inverted *v* formations in his writing (see Specimen 7), most frequently found in *m*, *n*, and *r*, and the last portion of *h*.

Specimen 7

81

EXPRESSIVE *ep* This often means putting into words, but also means revealing, showing. Thus, when a Graphoanalyst refers to an expressive nature, he does not necessarily mean a talkative one. This is evaluated when the writing shows both an emotionally reactive slant and talkativeness. When the writer is reticent, he may still show his feelings through the expression on his face or gestures such as a shrugged shoulder. How expressive the writer is may be determined from the degree of slant and the amount of inhibiting traits in evidence.

EXTRAVAGANT *e* An individual who is wasteful lacks a reasonable sense of values. His writing will show excessive generosity, no conservatism, and often a great love of variety with a highly developed imagination.

EXTROVERT *e* A person who is more interested in his environment and other people than himself, who is active and expressive, writes with a forward slant and makes large lower loops, showing active imagination. There will be an absence of clannishness and of strokes showing inhibition, timidity, and self-consciousness.

EXUBERANT *e* One meaning of this is effusive (see definition under "effusive"), but also can mean overflowing with good health and spirits. Such a person writes with a forward slant with energetic, forceful, forward-flowing strokes. An upward slant, denoting optimism, and long *t* crossings, showing enthusiasm, are often evident.

F

FACETIOUS *ep* This involves a sense of humor, which is indicated by initial flourishes that are not ostentatious, and is frequently accompanied by light sarcasm (cross strokes that taper to a fine point, but are not heavy).

The initial strokes on "found" and "men" in Specimen 1 indicate a sense of humor, and the *t* crossings show light sarcasm. The young woman who wrote this frequently made facetious remarks when she contributed to group discussions.

Specimen 1

FACILE *e* One interpretation of this is "easily persuaded"; when used in this sense yielding strokes and lack of definiteness will be evident in the writing. When used to mean fluent, as a facile mind, fluidity of thought will be evident. See "dexterity", "dexterous".

FACULTY *e* Power or ability to do some special thing. Refer to "talent".

FAILURE. Actual failure does not show in handwriting. The term is relevant; an individual can believe that he is a failure, yet be considered quite successful by others. A person can be a failure socially, or in personal ad-

83

justment, and at the same time be a success in the business world, or vice versa. All extremely emotional people undergo a feeling of failure at times, and this is enhanced when they are also pessimistic.

FAINTHEARTED *e* See "timid".

FAIR, FAIR-MINDED *e* Just and honest; unprejudiced. This is determined by a slant (see Specimen 2), showing a poised, judicial nature, accompanied by broad-mindedness and lack of deceit.

an impartial individual

Specimen 2

FAITHFUL *e* A trustworthy, loyal person shows loyalty to ideals by making small round dots over *i* and *j*. Lack of deceit will be evident, and this is shows when the circle letters (*a, o, g,* etc) are made open or simply closed at the top without an initial loop. Narrow lower loops are more often noticed than are the large, long ones that indicate love of variety.

FAITHLESS *e* Disloyal. Look for the opposite indications of those listed under "faithful".

FALLIBLE Every human being (including a Graphoanalyst) is likely to be erroneous or inaccurate at times, to be mistaken or deceived. Infallibility is an ideal toward which Graphoanalysts do strive, however.

FALSE, FALSITY *p* Refer to "deceit", "deceitful".

84

FANATICAL *e* A person who is unreasonably enthusiastic or overly zealous writes with an exaggerated number of sweeping cross strokes on his *t's* and with a forward slant. When excessively large upper loops are also in evidence, the writer is often a religious fanatic.

FANCIFUL *e* Indulging in fancies; imaginative. This is determined when light *t* crossings are made above the *t* stem (visionary, day-dreamer) and loops are large (imagination), particularly upper loops. Frequently there are breaks between the letters of a word (psychic).

FASTIDIOUS *e* Not easy to please; very critical. Writing of such a person will reveal strong analytical ability and an investigative mind, often accompanied by resentment, sarcasm, and irritability.

FATIGUED *e* A person who is physically or mentally exhausted lacks the coordination to function smoothly; therefore, the writing will be jerky or shaky. The same thing is true in senility, when decomposition of the muscle and nerve cells takes place.

FATUOUS *e* Silly, foolish people write with a lack of definiteness, purpose (will power), determination, and persistence, and usually show no sense of values.

FAULTLESS. A perfect human being would write with a complete absence of strokes indicating negative traits, but since no such person exists, such writing will not be found.

FEARFUL *e* A self-conscious person is afraid to talk or to appear in front of others for fear he will be embarrassed; the shy, timid person will be embarrassed, also.

Self-consciousness is evident when the last hump of an *m* or *n* is higher than the first strokes of the letter. Letters will be crowded, with frequent retracing, and the secrecy of a reticent person is often observed in the writing.

FEARLESS *e* Writing will show an absence of traits mentioned under "fearful"; initiative and self-confidence will be present.

FECKLESS *e* Refer to "careless".

FEEBLE-MINDED *e* The writing of a mentally weak person will lack evidence of comprehension, definiteness, a good memory, or strong will power.

FERVENT *ep* Having or showing great warmth of feeling; ardent. This is indicated when the writing shows extreme emotional expression, indicated in Specimen 3. Enthusiasm and deep emotions are usually present.

Specimen 3

FICKLE *e* Changeable or unstable in affection, interest, etc. Long lower and upper loops, extending into the line or writing below and above, showing strong desire for variety, and a changeable slant of the strokes, showing emotional instability, will characterize the writing of such a person.

FIDELITY *e* Faithfulness. Refer to "faithful".

FIERY *ep* One with a fiery nature is easily stirred up, excitable. This is basically determined by extreme emotional responsiveness. Sensitivity to criticism, temper, and resentment are all contributing factors.

FINESSE *e* The ability to handle difficult situations skillfully and diplomatically is revealed in the sharp points denoting comprehension combined with the tapering writing that shows diplomacy. Deceit is also often in evidence.

FIRE-EATER *e* The writing of a hot-tempered person who is always ready to quarrel or fight will reveal emotional reactiveness, strong temper, talkativeness, aggressiveness, sensitivity to criticism, and sarcasm.

FIRM *p* Showing determination. Refer to "determination".

FLAIR *e* A natural talent or ability. Refer to "talent".

FLASHY *ep* A showy person will embellish his writing with excessive flourishes and decorative strokes.

FLEXIBLE *ep* When one can be easily persuaded or influenced, his writing will have numerous yielding strokes with an absence of positiveness or strong will power and determination.

FLIRTATIOUS *p* To play at love or to toy with ideas without sincerity. This is primarily determined in flourished *d's*.

Specimen 4

FLUENCY *ep* The ability to write or speak easily, smoothly, and expressively. Fluidity of thought or speech will be the first trait to look for in the writing. The writer will be emotionally expressive, and comprehensive. If the ability is in relation to writing, look for figure-eight *g's*, Greek *e's*, and/or delta *d's*; if it is in relation to speaking, look for open-mouthed circle letters.

FLUIDITY *p* The quality of being able to change rapidly or easily. In Graphoanalysis, this term is used in connection with thought or speech. Fluidity of thought or speech implies the ability to change one's thoughts or speech from one subject to another with ease and rapidity. It is evidenced in flowing strokes such as are found in an *f* (see Specimen 5) when the lower loop is reversed and in the figure-eight *g*.

ning after four

Specimen 5

FOGY *ep* A person who is overly conservative will compress all of his strokes and leave very narrow spaces between words and stroke combinations. Narrow-mindedness will be evident.

FOOLISH *e* Refer to "fatuous".

FOPPISH *e* A vain man who pays too much attention to his appearance writes with a heavy stroke (love of colors, good clothes, etc.) and makes extremely high *t* and *d* stems (vanity). Shallowness and lack of sincerity will accompany this trait.

FORCEFUL *e* This adjective can be applied to one who writes with a vigorous, forward-moving stroke; initiative, aggressiveness, strong will power and determination, and positiveness will be present.

FORGERY *e* To be able to detect counterfeit documents and signatures with a high degree of success, a Graphoanalyst needs to study the advanced course in Graphoanalysis. Too many details are involved to be presented here.

FORGETFUL *e* The person who has a poor memory reveals this by not paying attention to details; he forgets to cross his *t's* and dot *i's* and *j's*. He also shows a lack of forceful characteristics.

FORMAL *e* One who behaves in accordance with prescribed customs, who is stiff and prim, writes in a similar manner. He will make tall, retraced *t* and *d* stems, showing pride and the desire to conform, showing dignity. There will be marked conservatism and the slant will be near-vertical. Close attention to details will be evident in precisely dotted *i's* and carefully crossed *t's*.

FORTHRIGHT *ep* Straightforward; frank. This is primarily determined by circle letters (*a, o, g,* etc., as shown in Specimen 6) that are either open at the top or are simply closed with no loops in them. Desire for simplicity and directness is usually present; this is evident when a simple downstroke is used rather than a loop or a stem on such letters as *t, b,* etc.

[handwriting specimen]

Specimen 6

FORWARD *e* A pushing, presumptuous writer shows initiative or aggression and is overly self-confident.

FOUNDATION, EMOTIONAL. The fundamental principle on which an individual's personality is based is his emotional foundation. How emotionally expressive and reactive he is to situations or to other people is determined by the slant of his writing. The farther it slants to the right, the greater is the writer's emotional reaction and expression. Another facet of the emotional foundation is the depth or endurance of his feelings: how deeply he is affected by emotional incidents and how long he continues to carry an emotion. This is determined by the heaviness of the strokes, or the width of them. See "depth of emotions". Just as a person's emotional foundation is modified by other traits, so are all other traits present affected by this foundation.

90

FOUNDER OF GRAPHOANALYSIS See "Bunker, M. N."

FOUR-FLUSHER *ep* Refer to bluff, bluffer.

FRACTIOUS *p* Peevish, irritable. This is evident when *i* and *j* dots are made with a jab of the pen (see Specimen 7). It is sometimes shown in short, arrow-like *t* crossings that fall to the right of the *t* stem.

Specimen 7

FRANK *p* The outspoken, candid writer makes the small circle letters, *a, o, g,* etc., as illustrated in Specimen 8, in such a manner that they are open at the top. Frankness is also indicated in an *e* made like a circle, not narrow and elongated.

Specimen 8

FRAUD *p* See "deceit".

FRETFUL *ep* Querulous, irritable. This is primarily determined from *i* dots (and *j* dots) that are jab strokes as
shown in Specimen 9; talkativeness is usually present.

Specimen 9

FRIENDLY *e* Look for such characteristics as generosity
and a sympathetic nature, and a lack of self-interest,
vanity and ostentation.

FRIGID *ep* The person who is without warmth of feeling
or manner, who is stiff and formal, writes with a vertical
or backhand slant, with little depth to the strokes. Usually
t's and *d's* will be tall and retraced and marked conservatism will be present.

FROSTY *ep* Cold in manner. Refer to "frigid" above.

FRUGAL *e* A person who does not spend freely, who is
economical, shows this trait in compressed writing, a
lack of long, extravagant finals or wide spacing between
strokes. Frugality does not rule out generosity; it implies
that a person does not spend or give unnecessarily, that
he is not wasteful.

Specimen 10 is the writing of a woman who was known
to be very good-hearted, but she was, at the same time,
extremely careful about how she spent her money or her
time.

Specimen 10

FURIOUS *ep* Full of violent anger or intense feeling. Primarily this is shown in an extremely emotionally reactive slant with very heavy strokes (see Specimen 11). High temper will be evident in the slashing, pointed *t* crossings that slant downward, or in tick strokes. There will frequently be resentment, sarcasm, and sensuality.

Specimen 11

FURTIVE *e* A sly, shifty individual shows in his writing such traits as secretiveness, deceit, lack of directness, lack of loyalty and lack of decisiveness.

FUTURE This is something that absolutely cannot be determined by handwriting analysis. Through assessment of the personality characteristics of an individual, a Graphoanalyst understands how the writer is likely to react in given circumstances, but in no case can he ever state that the individual will do a certain, specific thing in the future.

93

G

GABBLER *e* A person who talks rapidly and incoherently shows marked talkativeness in his writing, with an absence of self-control and cool judgment. Confusion of interests is often evident.

GABBY *p* Talkative. This is determined by frequent open-mouthed circle letters.

The girl who wrote Specimen 1 was known as a veritable chatterbox. She rarely closed the circle in her *o's* and *a's*.

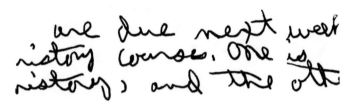

Specimen 1

GADABOUT *ep* One who goes about looking for fun and excitement naturally shows a great deal of love of change and variety in his writing. He likes to be on the go all the time, has many different interests. This is determined by frequent long loops that may even run into other lines of writing. Large *p* loops, indicating a desire for physical activity, are often present.

Specimen 2 is the writing of a young man who enjoyed running around so much that he failed to make grades high enough to keep him in college. He had the mental ability to do college work, but he was too interested in

94

having fun.

Specimen 2

GALLERY-PLAYING *e* Trying to win applause or approval by obvious means. This is determined when the writing shows ostentation and love of responsibility. Shallowness and pride or vanity are frequently present. Ostentation is revealed in excessive flourishes or decorative strokes; love of responsibility is shown by large initial circle loops, particularly on capital letters; shallowness is in basin-like *t* bars and shallow points on *m* and *n*; pride and vanity in tall *t* and *d* stems.

GAUCHE *e* Tactless. Look for bluntness and self-consciousness with absence of diplomatic ability.

GENEROUS *p* Willing to give or share; unselfish. This includes willingness to give time and energy as well as money or material things. It is determined by long finals on stroke combinations (see Specimen 3) and wide spacing between letter combinations.

Specimen 3

GENIAL *e* One with a cheerful, friendly, and sympathetic nature writes with a forward slant, showing he is sympathetic or emotionally responsive. His writing will slant upward, showing optimism. Love of change and variety and a good sense of humor are often present, but there will be a lack of resentment, irritability, and the tendency to domineer.

GENIUS *e* Great mental capacity or great and original creative ability in some art, science, etc., must be determined through evaluation. It may depend primarily upon unusually keen comprehension or on outstanding talent indications.

GENTLE *e* When a person is generous and kind, his writing will show a sympathetic nature and generosity with a lack of harsh qualities such as resentment, temper, the desire to domineer, and sarcasm.

GIFTED *e* Refer to "talented".

GLIB *e* Speaking in a smooth, easy manner. This characteristic is determined when talkativeness and diplomatic ability are evident in the writing; bluntness and self-consciousness will be absent.

GLOOMY, GLUM *ep* A person who looks on the dark side of life writes with a downward slant, showing pessimism. This is usually accompanied by the emotional slant of a very reactive nature.

GOAL *p* An object or end that one strives to attain; aim. What one's goals are cannot be pin-pointed by Graphoanalysis; where one placed his goals can be. This is determined by the position of his *t* crossings on the stem of the *t*. When they are very low, near the level of small letters, the writer has no ambition. The higher on the stem they are placed, the farther ahead are his goals placed. When they are so high that they are above the *t* stem, the writer places them so far ahead that they are not practical goals, but rather visionary ones.

The writer of Specimen 4a had no long term goals; he was more concerned with immediate goals than with future ones. The writer of Specimen 4b was more ambitious, but still practical in his goal setting. Specimen 4c represents the visionary goal setter, whose aims are not practical.

Specimen 4

97

amy of the other senses
question about determine

b

what the story

c

GO-GETTER *e* Although this is a slang expression, it is commonly used to describe one who usually gets what he wants. Such a person shows initiative and aggressiveness in his writing, plus positiveness, will power, persistence, and determination.

GOOD-NATURED *e* A pleasant, agreeable nature is revealed by absence of such traits as resentment, irritability, temper, bluntness, aggressiveness, sarcasm, a tendency to domineer, and pessimism.

GOSSIPY *e* A person who is inclined to chatter, to repeat rumors about others, shows excessive talkativeness (open-mouthed circle letters) in his writing, along with an active imagination (large loops on *g, y,* and *j*) and a curious mind (inverted *v* points on *m, n,* etc.). Sarcasm and analytical ability are also often evident.

GRAPHOLOGY An unstandardized method, largely intuitive, of attempting to read human physical and mental conditions, and frequently the future, from handwriting. Lacking uniform principles or fundamentals, graphology includes all handwriting analysis methods, both honest and fraudulent, outside the standardized science of Graphoanalysis. Determinations in Graphoanalysis are based on the results of years of intensive research. The coined word "Graphoanalysis" is a registered trademark.

GRASPING, GREEDY *p* Wanting excessively to have or acquire is shown in a great number of initial hooks, large or small.

Specimen 5

GREGARIOUS *e* One who is fond of the company of others is determined when the writing shows large lower loops on *g, y,* and *j* (love of change and variety, lack of selectivity or clannishness), the forward slant of an emotionally responsive person, and lack of conservatism and other inhibiting traits.

GRIM *e* A merciless, unyielding, harsh person does not reveal a sympathetic or emotionally responsive nature, nor generosity. No yielding, submissive strokes will be evident, but there is usually narrow-mindedness.

GRUFF, GRUMPY *e* Bad-tempered. Look for marked irritability and temper, lack of sympathetic and friendly indications.

99

GUARDED *ep* Cautious, careful, restrained. This is determined through strokes showing caution and marked conservatism. Secretiveness is more predominant than frankness in such a person.

GULLIBLE *e* When a person can be easily cheated or tricked, his writing will show that he is easily influenced; it will lack keen comprehension, analytical ability, and decisiveness.

GUSHY *e* Refer to "effusive".

H

HANDWRITING. Although this means, technically, writing done by hand, the term Graphoanalysis is used to cover any writing, even though the pen is held in the toes or the teeth. No matter what method of holding the pen is used, mental habits, individual characteristics, reveal themselves in the strokes of the writing.

HANDY *e* Refer to "dexterous".

HAPPY *e* This is an emotional state to which some natures are more inclined than others. It is more likely to apply to the optimist with a good sense of humor than to the pessimist; to the emotionally expressive person than to the cool, reserved one. Although it is greatly affected by external stimuli, an optimistic person more often finds happiness in an unfavorable environment than another person does in a favorable one.

HARD, HARD-BOILED, HARD-HEARTED *e* These all refer to the person who is unfeeling, not easily moved by sentiment, and are indicated by vertical or backhand writing with light lines, with no yielding strokes or generosity.

HASTY *ep* Impetuous or short-tempered. The former primarily is determined in writing with a forward slant, and without restraining influences such as conservatism, the writer will naturally be impulsive. When the latter definition is applicable, jab strokes for *i* and *j* dots, tick strokes, and pointed *t* crossings that fall to the right of the *t* stem show the writer's irritability and short temper.

In Specimen 1 both impulsiveness and irritability are evident.

Specimen 1

HAZY *e* Confused, indefinite thinking is revealed in stroke endings that become lighter or weaker (indecisiveness) and loops that interfere with writing on lines above and below the line (confusion of interests). Weak goal-setting and poor comprehension are often evident.

HEALTHY *e* This implies normal physical and mental vigor, freedom from disease, disorder, etc. The actual physical strength of a writer is not revealed in normal writing, but some debilitating illnesses do affect the writing. It becomes shaky, with many corrugated lines. Graphoanalysts do not, however, diagnose specific illnesses from handwriting. Mental and emotional strength is revealed by the way the strokes are made, and can be determined by evaluation.

HEARTLESS *e* One meaning of this is lacking in spirit, courage, or enthusiasm, and is determined by lack of enthusiasm, initiative, or aggressiveness. Another meaning is without kindness, unfeeling, in which case the writing will show a cold nature, self-interest, stinginess, lack of emotional depth, and lack of generosity.

HEARTY *e* The writing of such an individual is characterized by an emotionally responsive slant, enthusiasm, and lack of inhibitions.

HEAVY When this term is used in Graphoanalysis in relation to the strokes in the writing, it is in reference to the pressure used on the pen. Heavy pressure results in wide strokes, and reveals deep, long-lasting emotions, just as light pressure results in light line writing, showing the opposite of heavy writing.

Because it takes a certain amount of pressure for anyone to use a ballpoint pen, it is more difficult to assess the relative heaviness and lightness of writing done with that instrument. Both Specimens 2a and 2b were written with ink pens. The first one shows comparatively heavy line writing; the second, very light.

right one, but will it

picture (Football) you can

with his swete brethe

in every holt & heth

Specimen 2

HECTIC *e* Characterized by confusion, haste, agitation. This is determined by high emotional reaction, often a varied slant, and confusion of interests (shown in loops so long that they interfere with writing on the lines above and below).

HEDONISTIC *e* Living a life of pleasure; self-indulgent. Sensuousness or sensuality will be evident, with no restraining influences. There will be a lack of generosity and conformity. Independence of thought and action will be evident.

HEEDFUL *e* Careful; attentive. Such a person is revealed in carefully dotted *i's* and *j's*, with the dot placed close to the point of the letter, precisely crossed *t's*, and long strokes at the end of the line denoting caution.

HELPFUL *e* A person who likes to be of service to others will show in his writing generosity and a sympathetic or emotionally responsive nature. Broad-mindedness and a love of responsibility are often indicated.

HENPECKED *e* The only way a Graphoanalyst could determine whether or not a man is henpecked would be by examining the writing of both him and his wife. If his writing showed a lack of forceful, dominant tendencies, and hers showed a strongly domineering nature, one could logically conclude that the man is domineered by his wife.

HIGH-MINDEDNESS *e* Having high ideals. This is shown when long upper loops (philosophical or spiritual imagination) are accompanied by honesty (lack of deceit), loyalty to ideals (small round dots for *i* and *j*), and other positive traits.

Note the tall, pointed loops on *h, k* and *l* in Specimen 3 (the *t* loops indicate sensitivity to criticism). This was written by a pre-ministerial student, who wanted to perform his life's work in the field of religion.

all I am going to the

to check on the total

Specimen 3

104

HIGH-STRUNG *ep* Nervous, excitable. This is determined primarily by a far forward slant, and is evaluated in relation to other traits present, such as irritability and temper or the lack of them.

HOGGISH *e* One who is both very selfish and greedy writes with a large number of initial hooks, showing a great desire to acquire, and the compressed strokes that show conservatism, with none of the long finals or spaces between words or stroke combinations that show generosity.

HONEST *ep* The person who is frank and open, who is straightforward and free from deceit, makes small circle letters such as *o, a,* and *g* either open at the top or as wide circles simply closed without loops inside them. This is reinforced by the presence of loyalty to ideals, and detracted from by an overly active imagination, excessive acquisitiveness, or other negative traits. Basically, though, it is determined by lack of deceit.

HOPEFUL *p* The optimistic person who goes on feeling that what is wanted will happen, even though hope seems baseless, shows this trait by slanting his writing upward (see Specimen 4). The tendency to be hopeful is also indicated in *t* crossings and final strokes that have an upward slant.

what is the time

Specimen 4

HOPELESS *p* This is an antonym of hopeful. Such a person does not expect a favorable outcome, and is therefore pessimistic. It is shown in the writing by a downward slant (see Specimen 5) of single words or of lines of writing.

Specimen 5

HOSTILE *ep* When a person is antagonistic toward others his writing reveals this primarily in marked resentment of and anticipation of imposition. This is determined by inflexible initial strokes going up from the base line to the letter. It is often accompanied by high sensitivity to criticism, the desire to domineer, active imagination, and stubbornness.

HUFFY *e* An easily offended person reveals this trait when his writing shows that he is quite sensitive to criticism (inflated *t* and *d* stems), resents being imposed on, is irritable, and is highly emotional.

HUMBLE *e* This means an unassuming character in which there is an absence of pride and assertiveness. The definition itself indicates that the humble writer will not show great pride or vanity; there will also be an absence of ostentation, love of responsibility, aggressiveness, and sensuality. Rather than domination, the writing will show submissiveness.

HUMILITY *e* Absence of pride or self-assertion. See "humble."

106

HUMOROUS *p* The person who has a sense of humor shows this in his writing by making initial flourishes that are not ostentatious. They may appear before many letters, but are usually most noticeable before capital *m's* and *n's* as shown in Specimen 6.

Specimen 6

HYPERCRITICAL *e* Too severe in judgment; hard to please. Such a person's handwriting will show extremely marked analytical ability, a judicious nature, an investigative mind, and, quite often, sarcasm and resentment.

HYPERSENSITIVE *p* Abnormally or excessively sensitive. Extremely inflated loops for *t* and *d* stems reveal this trait. The average (or normal) writer shows some sensitivity to criticism, but when nearly all of the *t's* and *d's* are made with large loops, even though they are not excessively large, the writer may be considered abnormally sensitive.

HYSTERICAL *ep* The writing of an emotionally uncontrolled person slants far to the right, showing an extremely emotionally reactive nature. The trait is emphasized when the writing is heavy, revealing the depth and endurance of the writer's feelings. It is decreased when inhibiting traits such as caution or secretiveness are present, or increased by temper, irritability, resentment, etc.

I

IDEALISTIC *e* Such a person is characterized by thinking based on his conception of things as they should be or as he would wish them to be – not materialistic. His writing will show a preponderance of upper loops over lower loops; his imagination will be more in the philosophical than the practical realm. There will be good comprehension and loyalty to ideals, and often visionary goal-setting.

IDIOSYNCRASY *p* Any personal peculiarity or mannerism. The person who likes to be different, to be individual in some way, shows this by making his *i* and *j* dots as circles instead of dots as shown in Specimen 1.

1952 .

jor in Social Science
Physical Education and

Specimen 1

IGNORANT *e* Lacking knowledge, education, or experience. This cannot be determined by handwriting alone; a person with very little formal education can know a great deal about many things; a person with marked intelligence can be lacking in experience. For this reason, competent analysts cannot use this term without extraneous information about the writer.

ILL, ILLNESS. Whether or not the writer of a specimen is unhealthy, is sick, cannot be determined from the writing except in cases where the illness affects the neural system, and thus affects the script of the writer. Even so, specific diseases cannot be diagnosed from the writing. The foregoing statements are based on research (or the lack of it) that has been done up to the present time, and do not rule out the possibility of further study and discoveries in this field in the future.

ILLEGIBLE. Handwriting that is very difficult or impossible to read as far as the connotation of the script is concerned is no drawback to determination of personal characteristics by Graphoanalysis, since the science is based on stroke values rather than letter or word values.

ILL-HUMORED *e* This is determined when such negative traits as resentment, irritability, pessimism, temper, and sarcasm are combined in the writing.

ILL-NATURED *e* Refer to "ill-humored."

ILL-TEMPERED *p* A bad remper is revealed in very heavy jab strokes for *i* and *j* dots, heavy jabbed, pointed *t* crossings that fall to the right of the *t* stem, and/or short, inflexible tick strokes at the beginning of stroke combinations.

IMAGINATION *p* The act or power of forming mental images of what is not actually present. This is revealed in large loops; the larger the loop, the more active is the imagination. Lower loops represent materialistic or practical imagination; upper loops, imagination in philosophical, theoretical, or spiritual fields.

The inflated loops in Specimen 2 shown below represent abnormally active imagination.

Specimen 2

IMAGINATIVE *p* Having, using, or showing imagination. See above.

IMMATURE *e* One who has not completely grown or developed mentally and emotionally, yet who is chronologically and physically mature, may still be considered immature, just as a child is immature. Variable emotional slant, weak, indecisive stroke endings, and many negative traits indicate a lack of emotional and mental maturity.

IMMODERATE. This means without restraint or excessive and can be applied to any individual trait that appears excessively in the writing, such as immoderate enthusiasm, immoderate generosity.

110

IMMORAL. This is a relative term, based upon the particular mores of the culture in which one lives; what is considered moral in one society may be considered immoral in another. Behavior that does not conform with the accepted standards of proper sexual behavior in one culture may be considered acceptable in another. Furthermore, the function of a Graphoanalyst is not to judge the character of a writer, but to interpret it without bias. For this reason, Graphoanalysts do not use this term in making personality assessments.

IMMOVABLE *e* The unyielding, unemotional person is determined when the slant is vertical or backhand and the stroke endings are blunt, showing decisiveness.

IMMUTABLE. It is very exceptional, practically impossible, to find a slant or a certain stroke that does not change or vary in a person's handwriting. That is why evaluation on the part of the Graphoanalyst is so important.

IMPARTIAL *e* A person who is unprejudiced or unbiased writes with a nearly vertical or vertical slant, showing a judicious rather than an emotionally reactive nature. Circle letters such as *e, o,* and *a* will not be narrow, but well-rounded, showing broad-mindedness.

Specimen 3 was written by a judge who was noted for his fair, impartial decisions. It is true that the circle portion of one *g* is closed with ink, but by far the majority of his circle letters in the complete specimen were circles, just as they are in this sample.

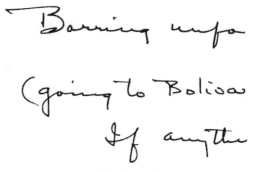

IMPASSIONED *e* Refer to "ardent."

IMPASSIVE *e* Not feeling or showing emotion. This does not necessarily connote that the writer cannot be affected by emotion, but rather that he does not show it. This characteristic is determined by near-vertical or vertical slant plus secretiveness (final loops inside circle letters, *a, o,* etc., that tie the letter shut), and lack of irritability, enthusiasm, and other traits that show an expression of feelings.

IMPATIENT *e* The writing of a person who feels or shows annoyance because of delay or opposition will show considerable irritability and impulsiveness.

IMPERIOUS *ep* An arrogant, domineering individual shows pride to the point of vanity in tall *t* and *d* stems (see Specimen 4), ostentation in unnecessary flourishes, and domineering proclivities in heavy, pointed *t* crossings that slant downward.

112

Specimen 4

IMPERTURBABLE *e* Refer to "impassive."

IMPETUOUS *ep* Acting suddenly with little thought; impulsive. This is applicable to the writer who has a forward slant without restraining influences such as caution or conservatism. Any emotionally responsive person, however, is going to react at times to emotional stimuli without stopping to think. The further the writing slants to the right, the more impulsive is the writer. Such a person may give or buy freely because of an emotional appeal, and then regret it later because he couldn't really afford to do so.

The young man who wrote Specimen 5 impulsively quit college to join the army. In a very few weeks, he wished he were back in college.

Specimen 5

IMPRACTICAL *ep* The person who is not realistic in goal setting crosses his *t*'s above the stem. Extremely low placement of *t* bars also indicates impracticality, in that the writer does not strive to do as much as he is able to do.

113

If he lacks imagination in the practical field, his writing will not show large lower loops.

Specimen 6 represents impracticality in goal setting. The writer daydreams about what he would like to do.

Specimen 6

IMPRESSIONABLE *e* The writer who is easily affected emotionally or intellectually is revealed by high emotional reaction accompanied by either depth of feeling or keen comprehension, or both.

IMPROVIDENT *e* Lacking foresight or thrift. This is determined by excessively long finals and spaces between stroke combinations (lack of a sense of values) plus very low or high placement of *t* bars (either one shows impracticality).

IMPULSIVE *ep* Refer to "impetuous."

INCOMPATIBLE *e* Not compatible. Refer to "compatible."

INCONSISTENT *ep* Changeable. This is determined primarily by a variable emotional slant; some strokes may go straight up and down, some backward, and some forward; also, some stroke combinations may slant upward and others downward. Any inconsistency in strokes indicates the appropriateness of using this adjective. Some *t* crossings may be very short and others very long, thus

114

the writer is not considtently enthusiastic, etc.

Note the great variation in slant of the upstrokes in Specimen 7.

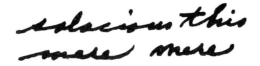

Specimen 7

INCONSTANT *e* One meaning of this is changeable. (See above). When used with the connotation of unsteady in affections or loyalties; fickle, there will be great love of change and variety, lack of loyalty, and, often, self-gratification. The light line writer is not necessarily any more fickle than the heavy line writer; evaluation of accompanying traits must be made. Pride, idealism, and loyalty all affect constancy.

INCONTINENT *ep* Without self-restraint, especially in regard to sexual activity. This is determined by gross sensuality (see Specimen 8) with lack of self-control.

Specimen 8

INCOORDINATION *e* Lack of coordination is shown in lack of rhythm, smoothness, and in unequal spacing and jerky strokes.

INCURIOUS *e* When a person is not interested in finding out about things, his writing will show a complete lack of investigative, exploratory ability, a lack of comprehension and analytical ability.

INDECISIVE, INDECISIVENESS *p* The individual who is characterized by indecision is revealed in weak finals on strokes (see Specimen 9). Such people lack definiteness and positiveness in their mental approach to life.

Specimen 9

INDEFINITE, INDEFINITENESS *p* Determined exactly as "indecisive," "indecisiveness."

INDEPENDENT *ep* A person who thinks and acts in accordance with his own beliefs, regardless of influence or persuasion of others or of the customs of the society in which he lives, reveals this trait by making short *t* and *d* stems. Such stems may be either retraced or looped; it is the height of them in relation to the rest of the writing that determines the independent nature of the writer.

Specimen 10

116

INDIFFERENT *e* Having or showing no interest, concern, or feeling; apathetic. This is revealed when there is very little or no emotional responsiveness, very light depth of feelings, lack of investigative thinking, very low goal setting, and absence of such positive traits as strong will power, determination, and initiative.

The girl who wrote Specimen 11 showed no interest in class and was not concerned with the opinions of others nor with their problems.

Specimen 11

INDIRECT *e* The person who is not straightforward in his speech and actions shows deceit in his writing, often accompanied by diplomatic ability. Desire for simplicity and directness will be absent.

INDIVIDUALISM *p* This can mean either the living of one's life in one's own way without regard for others, or an individual peculiarity. The former meaning is applicable when extreme independence of thought and action are apparent; the latter, when circle dots are used for *i* and *j*, showing that the writer has some idiosyncracy.

Specimen 12 is representative of the first definition. Note that the *d* stems are scarcely higher than the circle part of the letters, and the *t* stems are equally short.

117

fewer and can't wait
out and for summer
get a mad desire

INDOMITABLE *e* Not easily discouraged, defeated, or subdued. This trait is evident when *t* crossings grow heavier at the end of the stroke and downstrokes grow heavier (increasing will power and determination in face of opposition), when numerous tie strokes are in evidence. Optimism also frequently accompanies these traits.

INDULGENT *e* When one is indulgent toward others, there is a combination of yielding, submissive strokes, weak will power, and generosity. When one is self-indulgent, he gratifies his own desires and impulses; the writing will show sensuousness or sensuality with a lack of restraining influences.

INEXPRESSIVE *ep* One who is not expressive does not show his feelings. Such a person is revealed by a near-vertical, vertical, or backhand slant, which is usually accompanied by reticence.

INFERIORITY COMPLEX This is a psychological term that should be understood by Graphoanalysts. It refers to a neurotic condition resulting from feelings of inferiority; such feelings may derive from some physical inadequacy (either real or imagined) or from situations experienced in early childhood. The complex is often manifested in

118

excessive aggressiveness or a domineering attitude.

INFLEXIBLE *e* Firm in mind or purpose; stubborn; unyielding. Look for strong will power, strong determination,
stubbornness, definiteness, and absence of yielding strokes
in the writing.

INFLUENTIAL *ep* Having or exerting influence. This is
primarily based on evidence of enthusiasm in the writing.
The person who is enthusiastic is able to exert influence
on others because of the contagious effect of his ardent
interest. Besides evaluating the strength and endurance
of the enthusiasm, other traits such as comprehension,
definiteness, and depth of feelings must be considered.

INGENIOUS *e* Although this orginally meant having great
mental ability, it is now more commonly used to infer
cleverness or orginality in making or doing something.
The writing of an ingenious person will show good comprehension plus creative ability, often accompanied by
strong analytical ability.

INHIBITED *p* Such a person restrains or suppresses actions, emotions, or thoughts, and reveals this trait in
compressed writing with narrow spaces between letter
formations. Upstrokes on *m, n,* and the lower part of
h often retrace the previous downstroke.

Notice in Specimen 13 how frequently *n's* and *h's* are
squeezed, and how narrow is the space between most of
the letter formations in relation to the size of the script.
It was necessary for the girl who wrote this to have many
counseling sessions before she was able to express her
real thoughts and emotions about any but superficial
subjects.

119

child can pit his

opinion against

Specimen 13

INITIATIVE *p* The characteristic of orginating new ideas
or methods; ability to think and act without being urged.
This is determined by a forward-swinging stroke in *p*, *g*,
j and *y*, and also in the type of *t* illustrated in Specimen
14. Initiative lacks the force that is required for aggressiveness. Refer to "enterprise."

put gag many

Specimen 14

INQUISITIVE *p* The person who is eager to learn reveals
this by making inverted *v* strokes on *m*, *n*, and other
letters. No matter in what letter the inverted *v* is found,
the interpretation of it remains the same.

Specimen 15 was written by a middle-aged woman
whose inquisitive mind finds satisfactions in attending
adult education classes and various study groups. Note
how often the inverted *v* formation appears in this small
specimen.

120

Specimen 15

INSECURE, INSECURITY *e* Just as feelings of insecurity may be based on various causes, so do insecure people reveal their feelings of anxiety in different ways in their handwriting. In some instances, it is shown in self-consciousness; it is evident when timidity, resentment, oversensitivity to criticism, or great acquisitiveness are shown. In many cases, the desire to domineer, the tendency to bluff, or the desire to attract attention are based on feelings of insecurity.

INSINCERE *ep* Deceptive or hypocritical. This is determined primarily by intentional deceit; it may be accompanied by shallowness of thinking and/or diplomatic ability.

INSTABILITY *ep* Lack of stability, emotionally, is indicated by a variable slant of the writing; lack of determination is shown in weak downstrokes; irresolution is shown in weak final stroke endings.

INTELLECTUAL *e* This is applicable to a person of keen intelligence who is interested in advanced fields of knowledge. Such a person is determined when there is a com-

121

bination of unusually great mental powers and a desire for culture.

INTELLIGENT *e* Although one meaning of this is having or showing a high intelligence; quick to learn, there are many types of intelligence. The fast thinker, with instant, keen comprehension reveals this in needle-like points on *m*, *n*, *h*, etc. This does not mean that the slower thinker, the one who makes well-rounded *m's* and *n's*, is not just as intelligent in his own way. The rate of speed at which one thinks is not the determining factor in intelligence, even though intelligent is more often used in reference to the fast thinker. Creative ability is one form of intelligence. Personality traits that have been found by psychologists to have a high correlation with intelligence are determination, persistence, and conscientiousness.

INTENSE *ep* Having strong emotions is shown in broad, heavy strokes, regardless of the slant of the writing. Showing strong emotions is relevant when the strokes are heavy and the writing slants to the right.

INTERPRETATIVE, INTERPRETIVE *p* In Graphoanalysis this is used primarily in relation to an innate ability to understand and appreciate the real meaning of music, but can sometimes be applied to other arts. It is determined when there are frequent breaks between letter formations (see Specimen 16). In some cases such breaks can be interpreted as psychic ability.

Specimen 16

122

INTERVIEW. Meeting a person face to face in conference has been widely used (and still is) as a method of personality assessment, particularly by employers, personnel directors, and guidance counselors. Although the interview does have merit as a tool in personnel selection, particularly when personal appearance is important to a job, it does lack one important thing that Graphoanalysis has: the way an individual thinks and behaves is much more clearly revealed in his handwriting than it is in an interview.

INTOLERANT *e* The individual who is unwilling to tolerate others' opinions or religious beliefs shows narrow-mindedness and vanity in his writing. He is often dominating and self-interested.

INTRACTABLE *e* When a person is hard to manage, his writing reveals stubbornness and definiteness, frequently combined with temper and resentment.

INTROVERT *e* A person whose tendency is to direct his interest upon himself rather than external objects or events shows in his writing self-consciousness, inhibitions, timidity, and selectivity or exclusiveness in regard to friends.

INTUITIVE *p* This refers to knowing or learning something instantaneously without conscious use of reasoning, and is determined by frequent breaks between letters. See Specimen 16.

INVENTIVE *e* The ability to invent is indicated in a combination of creative ability, analytical ability, and active imagination. Creative ability is revealed in broad or flat-topped *m's, n's,* and *r's,* and sometimes in a combination of this stroke with the needle-like comprehension points.

Analytical ability is shown in v formations at the base line. Active imagination is evidenced by large loops; such upper loops indicate imagination in theoretical or philosophical fields; lower ones in material or practical areas.

INVESTIGATIVE p See "exploratory."

IRASCIBLE p An easily angered person shows great irritability to the point of temper. Heavy, jabbed i and j dots are the most common indications of this, but it is also revealed in tick strokes and t crossings that are jabs or pointed strokes that fall to the right of the t stem. This word is a synonym of irritable, but infers more anger than annoyance.

IRRITABLE p Easily annoyed or provoked. This is indicated by the frequent use of irregular short dashes or arrow-like jabs for dots over i and j (see Specimen 17). If the strokes are light, they indicate that the writer possesses light irritability, that he recovers from the feeling of annoyance in a short time. If they are heavy, the reverse is true.

Specimen 17

124

J

JEALOUS *p* The writer who is either resentfully suspicious of a rival or resentfully envious of others reveals this trait by making small, squared or cramped initial loops as shown in Specimen 1.

Specimen 1

JOCOSE, JOCULAR *ep* A humorous, facetious person who likes to joke is determined primarily by the initial flourish that indicates a sense of humor (see Specimen 2). Light sarcasm, talkativeness, optimism, and emotional expressiveness often accompany this sense of humor.

Specimen 2

JOINER *e* A person who is given to joining various organizations is extrovertive. His writing will show marked love of change and variety (large lower loops), even to the point of a confusion of interests, and an emotionally responsive slant. Large initial loops, indicating love of responsibility, are often evident.

JOVIAL *ep* Refer to "jocose," "jocular."

JUDGMENT *ep* Power of comparing and deciding. This is most frequently used in Graphoanalysis with an adjective: cool judgment or unbiased judgment, and is primarily applicable to the writer whose slant registers no further to the right on the emotional gauge than B-C. See Specimen 3. When this near-vertical or vertical slant is accompanied by analytical ability and absence of extravagance or exaggeration, one can well assume that the writer bases actions and decisions more on objective judgment than on emotional impulses.

one stated in the a text. It goes someth

Specimen 3

JUDICIAL *ep* Unbiased; carefully considering the facts, arguments, etc. Refer to "judgment."

JUDICIOUS *e* Wise and careful. Look for the near-vertical or vertical slant, analytical ability, comprehension, and caution.

JUST *e* The impartial person writes with near-vertical or vertical slant, shows broad-mindedness, and lack of deceit. Refer to "fair."

JUVENILE *e* See "immature."

K

KEEN *p* Sharp, penetrating. When this is used in reference to the mind, the mental acuteness of the writer is revealed in needle-like strokes in *m, n, r,* etc.

Specimen 1 is that of a seventy-year-old woman who was formerly a school teacher and who is still very alert mentally. Because of her keen intellect, she completed a master's degree at a very early age. Note that the last sections of her h's and n's form very sharp points.

Specimen 1

When this same adjective is applied to sarcasm, *t* crossings show extremely sharp points. Such a writer employs very cutting sarcasm. See Specimen 2 under "sarcastic."

KILL-JOY *e* When the writer is domineering, pessimistic, and narrow-minded, he is the type of person who will lessen other people's enjoyment.

KIND, KINDLY *e* This is applicable to the writer who has a sympathetic nature and generosity, and a lack of harsh qualities such as domineering tendencies and cutting sarcasm.

L

LACKADAISICAL *e* Showing lack of interest or spirit. This is revealed by a complete absence of enthusiasm, initiative, definiteness, and energetic forward-moving strokes of the pen.

LAGGARD *e* A backward or slow person writes with deliberateness (see Specimen 6 under deliberate) and a lack of impulsiveness and initiative.

LANGUID *e* Without vigor or vitality; without interest or spirit; indifferent. This is quite similar in meaning to lackadaisical, and is determined in much the same way.

Specimen 1 is the writing of a very indifferent young woman. Emotional responsiveness is not high, she shows no enthusiasm, very weak will power, no eagerness for learning, and lack of definiteness in thinking and acting.

Specimen 1

LARGE-MINDED *ep* The individual who is liberal, tolerant, and broad-minded in his views reveals this primarily by an absence of compressed formations in circles and loops. *E's* will be well-rounded circles; *o's, a's,* etc., will be round rather than narrow. None of the writing will show the compressed strokes of a conservative person.

LASCIVIOUS *e* Characterized by lust or lewdness. Such a person's writing will show sensuousness or sensuality without pride or desire for culture or self-restraint.

LASTING Enduring. This is used in Graphoanalysis to describe different traits. Long lasting will power and enthusiasm are both determined by the length of the *t* bars; lasting determination is revealed in long down-strokes below the base line of writing; lasting emotions are revealed in heavy or broad strokes.

LATENT Lying hidden and undeveloped within a person, as a quality or power. Undeveloped ability can be discerned in writing when indications of talent are present, but they are not prominent enough to justify the conclusion that it obviously exists.

LAX *e* Not strict or exact; careless. Such a person's writing will be characterized by an absence of firmness, of definiteness, of strong determination, persistence, and pride. Lack of precision and attention to details will also be evident.

LEADERSHIP *e* The ability to lead is obvious when the writing shows enthusiasm, rapidity of thinking, pride, initiative, and a lack of self-consciousness and timidity.

LECHEROUS *ep* The individual who indulges his sexual desires excessively and without restraint shows sensuality in his writing, accompanied by a lack of restraining qualities such as conservatism, pride, and self-control.

LEGIBILITY Whether or not a person's handwriting can be read or deciphered easily has no bearing on determination of the writer's personality traits by a Graphoanalyst, because such determination is based upon the way he makes his strokes, not upon what he wishes to convey by his written words.

LEVEL-HEADED *e* Having or showing an even temper and sound judgment. Such a person's writing shows a cool, poised nature and a lack of temper.

The woman who wrote Specimen 2 is level-headed enough to handle well a full time job in personnel work, raise a child, do her own housework, and help her husband complete his education.

Specimen 2

LIABILITY Something that works to one's disadvantage. As a rule, there are certain traits that are considered to be liabilities, or negative traits. This is generally true of deceitfulness–yet, it is an asset to the person whose career is in the diplomatic field. No one trait can be considered in and by itself to be bad or good; it is the way the trait is used that determines whether it is an asset or a liability.

130

LIBERAL *ep* When this is used to mean generous it is determined by long finals and wide spacing between letters. When used to mean broad-minded, it is shown in well-rounded circle letters (see Specimen 3) with a lack of the compressed strokes of a conservative person.

Specimen 3

LISTLESS *e* Refer to "languid."

LITERARY *ep* This is used in Graphoanalysis to refer to a talent, to the ability of the writer to develop skill in writing literature. It is primarily determined by small *g*'s made like *8*'s and by Greek *e*'s as illustrated in Specimen 4. It is sometimes indicated by a delta *d*, one which ends with a stroke made up over the circle part of the *d* in such a way that it suggests a triangle. Whether the writer's ability lies in fictional, editorial, scientific, or other types of writing depends upon evaluation of the accompanying traits.

Specimen 4

131

LIVELY *ep* Active, vigorous. In Graphoanalysis, this can be used to apply to mental qualities only, because a person who is confined to a wheel chair physically can still reveal an animated personality. A lively imagination is shown in large loops, upper or lower; the former indicate active imagination in philosophical or theoretical fields, the latter in practical areas. The writer with an active mind shows keen comprehension and writes with a forceful, forward sweep to his strokes.

LOFTY *ep* When this is used in reference to the writer's ideals, the writing will show marked philosophical and spiritual thinking. When used with the connotation of over-proud or arrogant, *t's* and *d's* will be extremely tall (vanity); ostentation and the tendency to domineer wil often be present.

LOGICAL *ep* Using correct reasoning. The type of thinker who uses valid induction or deduction before coming to a conclusion reveals this primarily in well-rounded *m's, n's,* etc. Analytical ability, poise, and creative ability usually are present.

LONGHEADED *e* Having much foresight; shrewd. This is determined from a combination of keen comprehension (sharp needle points on *m, n, h,* etc.) and strong analytical ability (frequent *v* formations at the base line). Initiative and interpretive ability are often present.

LOOSE-TONGUED *e* The person who talks too much writes with many open-mouthed circle letters such as *a* and *o* and shows a lack of restraining traits such as caution and repression.

132

LOQUACIOUS *e* Very talkative. This is determined by the same indications as "loose-tongued."

LOUTISH *e* Clumsy and stupid. Look for lack of comprehension and absence of rhythm or coordination.

LOVABLE *e* When a person's writing shows that he is generous, sympathetic, loyal, and sincere, without any harsh qualities such as the tendency to domineer, one might refer to him as lovable. Careful evaluation of all traits present must be made, however.

LOVE. The capacity to love may be revealed in handwriting, but it is impossible to determine from handwriting whether or not one individual loves another individual.

LOYAL, LOYALTY *p* The individual who is faithful to ideals makes small, round dots for *i*'s and *j*'s (see Specimen 5). The position of the dots, whether they are near the points of the letters or far from them, has no effect on the interpretation of the dots as indicating loyalty.

Specimen 5

LUCID *e* The clearheaded, rational thinker shows good comprehension, analytical ability, and definiteness in his writing.

LUSTFUL *e* An individual who is characterized by a desire to gratify the senses (usually used to mean sexual desire) will write with a heavy, broad stroke; his writing may show either sensuousness or sensuality, and acquisitiveness will be evident.

M

MAD, MADNESS *e* Mentally ill or mental illness are terms preferred by psychologists today to describe this condition. The writing will show disorder and extreme emotional expression without control.

MAD-CAP *e* Reckless and impulsive. The writing of such a person will show impulsiveness without restraining influences such as conservatism, caution, or self-control.

MAGISTERIAL *e* Domineering; pompous. Look for the downward-slanting, arrow-like *t* bars that indicate the tendency to domineer plus exceedingly tall *t* and *d* stems indicating vanity.

MAGNANIMOUS *e* A noble-minded person who generously overlooks injury or insult will write with a lack of resentment, sensitivity to criticism, or vanity. His writing will show generosity and a sympathetic nature.

MAGNILOQUENT *e* The boastful individual who talks big shows these traits in his writing: talkativeness (open-mouthed small circle letters such as *o* and *a*), bluffing (very blunt, short downstrokes below the base line), vanity (very tall *t* and *d* stems), and ostentation (unnecessary flourishes).

MALE. It is impossible to determine accurately from handwriting the sex of the writer since many women possess and show so-called manly qualities, both in their behavior and in their writing.

MANAGERIAL *e* One who has the characteristics of a successful manager shows the following traits in his writing; organizational ability (equal balance of upper and lower loops, particularly noticeable in *f*), definiteness (blunt final stroke endings), and good comprehension (points on *m, n, r,* etc.). Analytical ability and initiative are frequently found, but there will be an absence of antagonistic qualities such as sarcasm, resentment, and the desire to domineer.

MASTERFUL *e* This implies such strength of personality that the writer is able to impose his will on others, and is determined by strong, enduring will power (heavy, long, *t* crossings) and definiteness of thinking (blunt finals on strokes).

MASTERMIND *e* A person of great intelligence who has the ability to plan or direct a group project shows keen comprehension along with strong analytical ability, initiative, and organizational ability.

MATERIALISTIC *ep* The person who is more concerned with material than with spiritual goals or values reveals this when his upper loops are, for the most part, short (see Specimen 1), and his lower loops are prominent.

for good looks

Specimen 1

135

MATTER-OF-FACT *e* The unimaginative, literal-minded writer is practical in his goal setting, lacks imagination in theoretical lines, and is conservative. He likes simplicity and directness rather than ostentation.

MATURITY *e* The state or quality of being fully developed. In Graphoanalysis this is used in reference to mental characteristics and has nothing to do with the chronological age of the writer. Mental maturity is determined by firm and well-formed strokes, no matter how individualistic the writing is; there will be an absence of weak lines. The emotionally mature writer has a fairly consistent slant, without extreme variations.

MEALY-MOUTHED *e* Not outspoken or blunt; euphemistic and insincere. This is shown in shallowness and a lack of frankness, definiteness, and simplicity. Diplomatic ability is usually marked.

MEAN *e* When used to denote miserly, it is determined by extreme conservatism (squeezed writing, narrow spaces between letter formations) plus marked acquisitiveness (frequent initial hooks). When the word is used to mean bad-tempered or malicious, there will be temper, sarcasm, and often the tendency to domineer.

MECHANICAL *ep* When a person has the ability to work with machinery or tools, *m's, n's,* and *r's* will be broad or flat-topped. This is enhanced when there is even spacing between stroke combinations (sense of rhythm, coordination) and closely dotted *i*'s and *j*'s (attention to detail).

Specimens 2a and 2b were written by people who have and use mechanical ability. The first was written by an industrial arts teacher who uses his spare time making furniture for his home. The second was written by a young man who works on automobile motors in a garage.

I am thirty-one we been married for have one child, a art old.

a

dreary, days-like only are they or but they make

b

Specimen 2

MEEK *e* When used to mean not inclined to anger or resentment the writing will show no signs of irritability, temper, or resentment. When used to denote tamely submissive, there will be frequent yielding strokes, weak finals to strokes, and weak will power. It can often be applied to one writer in both meanings of the word.

MELANCHOLY *e* The tendency to be sad, gloomy, or depressed is present in anyone whose writing shows extreme emotional reactions, since such a person's moods fluctuate from one state of emotion to another. It is accented when pessimism is obvious in the writing.

MELODRAMATIC *e* Such a person likes to be sensationally dramatic. His writing will show him to be extravagantly emotional and to possess showmanship or ostentation.

MEMORY *ep* This refers to the ability or power to retain in the mind past thoughts, images, ideas, etc. It is determined by *i* and *j* dots placed close to the point of the letter (see Specimen 3) and careful crossing of the *t's*.

Specimen 3

MENDACIOUS *p* False, untruthful. This involves deceit, and is determined when small circle letters such as *o* and *a* have both an initial and final loop in them.

The majority of the circle letter formations in Specimen 4 show the double loops indicating self-deceit and deliberate deceit of others. For this reason, one can deduce that the writer will definitely be mendacious at times.

Specimen 4

MENTALITY *e* The capacity, power or activity of the mind of a person is revealed in his handwriting. All handwriting registers mentality to some extent, since the ability to make connected strokes indicates some degree of mentality. Refer to "intelligent."

138

MERCENARY *e* When an individual is motivated by a desire for money or other gain, his writing will show acquisitiveness in frequent initial hooks, conservatism in compressed writing, with no long finals of generosity. Lower loops, indicating practical imagination, will be more prominent than the upper loops of the philosophical or spiritual-minded person.

MERCIFUL *e* A lenient, compassionate person has a sympathetic or emotionally responsive nature with generosity and a lack of negative qualities such as narrow-mindedness, resentfulness, sarcasm, etc.

MERCURIAL *e* The quick-witted, changeable writer shows an intensely emotionally responsive nature, fast thinking, and love of change and variety.

MERRY *e* A good sense of humor and optimism will be evident in such a person's writing. He will not be self-centered or overly conservative.

METICULOUS *ep* The person who is extremely careful about details reveals this in very carefully dotting his *i*'s and *j*'s close to the point of the letter and in precision of crossing *t*'s as shown in Specimen 5. Conservatism, pride, and dignity are usually present.

jump into this project in time to deliver it in

Specimen 5

METTLESOME *e* Full of spirit, courage, ardor. Look for enthusiasm, emotional responsiveness, emotional depth, definiteness, and self-reliance.

139

MILD *e* Not extreme in any way; not severe or harsh. A mild nature is revealed not only by an absence of harsh qualities such as sarcasm and temper, but by positive qualities such as enthusiasm, definiteness, and will power that appear in moderation only. The writing will be light line, never sensual.

MILQUETOAST *e* Any timid, shrinking, apologetic person. Yielding, submissive strokes will be prominent in the writing; there will also be self-consciousness, repression, and indecisiveness. Yielding strokes are sprawled, formless, such as are seen in the *s* that is no more than a hook. Self-consciousness is shown in *m's* and *n's* when the final stroke (hump) is higher than the rest of the letter. Repression is revealed in cramped or squeezed strokes. Weak endings on final strokes indicate indecisiveness, lack of definiteness.

MIND. There are many definitions of this noun. The one that is applicable to the statement that the mind determines the way strokes are made in handwriting is, that which thinks, feels, wills, etc., but it must be broadened to include the conscious and the unconscious together as a unit. When a Graphoanalyst refers to "a good mind," what is usually meant is that the writer is intelligent. In spite of all the various definitions, however, psychologists are still trying to determine what the mind really is and how it actually functions.

MINOR TRAIT. This can be applied to any trait that appears in a given handwriting to a lesser extent than other traits. When infrequent indications of a trait appear, one may conclude that the trait is not a major characteristic of the writer and is therefore referred to as a minor trait.

MISERLY *e* Greedy and stingy. This is determined by a combination of acquisitiveness (initial hooks) and extreme conservatism (tightly compressed strokes and narrow spacing between letters and words indicated in Specimen 6)--complete lack of generosity.

Specimen 6

MISLEAD, MISLEADING *p* Deceive, deceiving, or delude, deluding. When one is self-deceiving circle letters such as *a, o, g,* and *d* have an initial loop inside the circle. The deliberately misleading person makes both initial and final loops inside the circle letter. Talkativeness and active imagination often are present.

Specimen 7 was written by a highly successful (in terms of number of sales) salesman. Many of his customers found out later, much to their sorrow, that the interpretation of their contracts was not exactly the one presented to them by the salesman.

Specimen 7

141

MISREPRESENT *p* Give a misleading idea of. See "misleading."

MISTRUSTFUL *e* The person who is full of doubt of suspicion reveals this in a combination of analytical ability (*v* formations at the base line), jealousy (small, squared, or cramped initial loops), and alertness against imposition (inflexible initial strokes going up from the base line). Sensitivity to criticism and active imagination are often present.

MIXER *e* The person who has the ability to get along with others is considered a good mixer, and is determined by broad-mindedness, love of variety, emotional responsiveness, and lack of self-consciousness, over-sensitivity to criticism, irritability, sarcasm, and temper. A bad mixer is determined by the opposite traits.

MODERATE *e* Such a person avoids excesses or extremes. Besides being used to describe an individual, this adjective may be used to describe a trait when that trait is present in the writing but is not exaggerated, such as moderate enthusiasm, moderate determination, etc.

MODEST *e* An unassuming, proper, reserved individual's writing will show a desire to conform to socially acceptable standards of behavior (retraced *t* and *d* stems), conservatism (compressed writing with the retraced *t* and *d* stems), and a lack of vanity or ostentation.

MOODY *e* Subject to gloomy, sullen moods or changes of mood. Anyone who is extremely emotionally reactive (far forward slant) is subject to changes of mood; when such a person also shows pessimism in his writing (downward slant of stroke combinations or lines) he can definitely be described as a moody person.

MORAL *e* This implies conformity with generally accepted standards of goodness or rightness in conduct or character. The desire to so conform is revealed in tall, retraced *t* and *d* stems, but whether or not one is likely to do so depends upon other traits such as self-control, sensuality, impulsiveness, etc. Furthermore, because of the variations in individual concepts of morality and because of environmental circumstances, it is never the place of a Graphoanalyst to pass judgment upon the morality or immorality of any other individual.

MORDANT *ep* Biting or sarcastic, as speech or wit. When a sense of humor is combined with strong sarcasm, they could be considered to be productive of mordant wit. When light sarcasm is combined with humor, one is considered merely witty. Sarcasm is revealed in sharply-pointed *t* crossings, and whether it is called strong or light depends upon the heaviness or lightness of the cross stroke. A sense of humor is revealed in initial flourishes that are not ostentatious.

MOUSY *e* A quiet, timid person shows secretiveness, lack of talkativeness, in small circle letters that are closed with a final loop, and he shows timidity in compressed writing with self-consciousness (the last part of *m* and *n* higher that the rest of the letter).

Specimen 8 was written by a mousy student who never spoke up in class except when required to give a report. Notice the squeezed *m's* and *n's*, the higher final stroke on them, and how often *o's* are closed with a final loop.

Specimen 8

MUDDY. This adjective is used in Graphoanalysis to describe writing that is heavy, has blots, blurs, and corrugations. Circle and loop strokes are often clogged. Such writing indicates sensuality, and is not to be confused with the heavy, clean-cut strokes that indicate sensuousness.

MULTIPLICITY *p* This means a great number, and can be applied to interests when lower loops (except in *p*) are very long. It can also be applied to long upper loops except in the case of *t* and *d* loops.

The lower loops on *p's* indicate a mental desire for physical activity, but the other lower loops in Specimen 9 reveal the writer's multiplicity of interests.

Specimen 9

144

MUSICAL *ep* Fond of, sensitive to, or skilled in music. Whether or not the writer is skilled in music cannot be determined from the handwriting. However, one who is sensitive to and appreciative of music reveals this in frequent breaks between letter formations. When this is accompanied by a good sense of rhythm and creative ability, one may conclude that the writer possesses musical ability.

N

NAGGING *e* Continually finding fault, scolding, etc. This is determined by a combination of marked irritability, talkativeness, resentment, sarcasm, and analytical ability.

NARCISSISM *e* Self-love; excessive interest in one's own appearance, comfort, importance, abilities, etc. Such a person writes with a vertical to backhand slant; he makes exceedingly tall *t* and *d* stems (vanity); his writing is compressed and shows no generosity; narrow *e's, o's* and *a's* reveal his narrow-minded attitude toward others. His strokes often show sensuousness or sensuality.

NARROW, NARROW-MINDED *ep* The individual who is without breadth of view; prejudiced, is primarily determined by compressed *e's* and other small circle letters Self-consciousness and timidity may accompany this.

NATURAL *e* Free from affectation or restraint. Such a person likes simplicity and directness, shown when an initial downstroke is used instead of a loop on letters such as *b, f,* etc. The writing will not show inhibitions, repressions, nor ostentation.

NEGATIVE. In Graphoanalysis this term is applied to those traits that are considered liabilities to the individual; it is an antonym to positive. Isolated traits cannot be considered completely negative in themselves; it is the way such traits are used in combination with other traits that determines whether or not they are negative in any one person's character.

NERVOUS *e* Characterized by emotional tension, restlessness, agitation, etc. This is determined when the writer shows high emotional reaction and/or variable emotional reaction plus inhibitions, desire for change and variety, irritability, etc.

Specimen 1 was written by a man whose nervousness caused him to break out in a rash. He worked under great tension, and in spite of his timidity he was forced to deal with the public by the nature of his job.

Specimen 1

146

NOBLE *e* When a person has lofty ideals, large upper loops will be more prominent in the writing than lower loops, and will be accompanied by loyalty and generosity with a lack of deceitfulness, resentment, and other negative characteristics.

NONCHALANT *ep* Without warmth or enthusiasm. As shown in Specimen 2, this is determined by a vertical or backhand slant and short *t* crossings. Such a person shows a cool lack of concern for others.

Specimen 2

NORMAL. This implies conformity with an established norm or standard for its kind as in normal intelligence and can be used in reference to any trait as long as the Graphoanalyst has had sufficiently great experience in examining large numbers of specimens of writing to be able to judge the normal extent to which said trait appears in the average person's handwriting.

NOTIONAL *e* The writer who has visionary ideas makes *t* crossings that fall above the *t* stem.

The young man who wrote Specimen 3 was always having "a notion to do this," or "a notion to do that," but rarely did anything ever come of his notions.

Specimen 3

O

OBDURATE *p* One meaning of this is stubborn, in which case it is determined by a combination of strokes (see Specimen 1) that forms a wigwam as in *t, d,* etc.

Specimen 1

OBEDIENT *e* The writing of a docile, tractable, individual reveals yielding strokes and an absence of stubbornness, independence of thought and action, and positiveness.

OBSEQUIOUS *e* Overly submissive. Such a person's writing will show an excessive number of yielding strokes with no strong will power, independence, or definiteness.

148

OBSERVANT *ep* Paying careful attention; keenly watchful. This is determined by close dotting of *i's* and *j's* and careful attention to other details such as crossing *t's*, plus good comprehension.

The writer of Specimen 2 was observant enough to be able to make high marks on examinations with a minimum of time spent in study.

that in his own way Milton

Specimen 2

OBSTINATE *p* See "stubborn."

OBTUSE *e* Slow to understand or perceive; determined by an absence of strokes indicating comprehension.

OFFENSIVE *e* Causing resentment, anger, etc. This can result from various traits such as domineering tendencies (downward slanted, arrow-like *t* bars), vanity (excessively high *t* and *d* stems), sarcasm (sharply pointed *t* crossbars), bluntness (very heavy, short, blunt final strokes), marked irritability (jabbed strokes for *i* and *j* dots), etc.

OFFICIOUS *e* The person who offers unnecessary and unwanted advice or services to others is usually domineering, vain, and ostentatious. This is revealed in his writing in downward slanting, pointed *t* bars, extremely tall *t* and *d* stems, and unnecessary flourishes.

OPEN-MINDED *e* When one has a mind that is open to new ideas and is free from prejudice, the writing shows broad-mindedness and investigative, exploratory thinking.

149

OPINIONATED *e* The person who holds unreasonably to his own opinions shows tenacity, positiveness, narrow-mindedness, and stubbornness.

OPTIMISTIC *p* One who looks on the bright side of things reveals his hopeful attitude by the upward slant of his writing. Indications of this trait are also evident in upward-slanting finals and *t* crossings.

Specimen 3 is the writing of a philosophy professor whose own philosophy is basically an optimistic one.

Specimen 3

ORDERLY *p* This implies freedom from disorder or confusion and is closely related to organizational ability. Loops, especially in the letter *f*, will be equally balanced above and below the line (see Specimen 4), with no confusion with strokes in the lines of writing above and below.

Specimen 4

150

ORGANIZATIONAL ABILITY *p* The capacity for putting things or ideas in order is determined as is orderly.

Specimen 5

ORIGINATIVE *ep* Creative ability is revealed in broad, rounded, or flat-topped *m's, n's,* and *r's.* It can also be determined from a combination of keen comprehension and analytical ability with other traits.

The creative ability of the woman who wrote Specimen 6 can be deduced through evaluation. She writes poems for children. Note the good sense of rhythm, the figure-eight formations, the rounded *n's* and the indications of comprehension.

Specimen 6

OSTENTATIOUS *ep* The showy writer who likes to attract attention uses excessive flourishes, decorative strokes that comprise over-ornamentation of the writing (see Specimen

7). Vanity is often evident in the writing of such a person; it is revealed in excessively tall *t* and *d* stems.

Specimen 7

OUTSPOKEN *p* A frank person frequently leaves circle letters, *o, a, g, d,* open at the top and makes circular *e's* rather than elongated or narrow ones. See Specimen 8 under "frank."

OUTSTANDING. Any trait that appears prominently or conspicuously in the writing may be considered an outstanding characteristic of the writer.

OVERBEARING *e* Arrogant, domineering tendencies are revealed in very tall *t* and *d* stems (excessive pride) and downward slanting, arrow-like *t* bars.

OVERCONFIDENT *e* The too confident individual makes frequent underscores, not only in his signature, but in other writing as well, and frequent, heavy, blunt, finals (overly positive), with a lack of other abilities necessary to back up this confidence.

152

OVERDRAWN *ep* Exaggerated. This is usually applied to the imagination and is determined when loops, either upper or lower, are excessively inflated. The lower loops in Specimen 8 may be termed overdrawn when they are considered in relation to the size of the rest of the writing.

*that is going on right now
ever is writing the peopl
only what they wanted
to say*

Specimen 8

P

PACIFIC *e* Refer to "calm."

PAINSTAKING *e* Very careful, shown in very close attention to details and conservatism.

PARADOX *e* A person who is inconsistent or contradictory in character or behavior. No human being is completely consistent in character or behavior, but some are more paradoxical than others. Almost all traits can appear inconsistently in handwriting. The same person can show both domination and submission, both warm emotional responsiveness and a cool, withdrawn nature, both frankness and deceit, both generosity and conservatism. . . and so on through other contradictory traits. When such a contradiction is strong in the writing, the writer can be considered paradoxical in relation to the traits concerned.

PARSIMONIOUS *p* Refer to "stingy."

PARTICULAR *e* This can mean either extremely careful or fastidious, and can be determined by precise crossing of *t's* and close dotting of *i's* and *j's* (attention to details), or frequent *v* formations at the base line (analytical thinking) plus this precision. When applied to selection of friends, lower loops on *g, y,* and *j* will be either very narrow or small square or circle loops.

PASSIONATE *p* Having or showing strong feelings. This often implies an impetuous kind of strong emotion. It is based on the heavy, broad strokes of sensuousness or sensuality (see Specimen 1). The slant can show either extremely intense emotional reaction or can be more nearly vertical with obvious suppression of emotions.

Specimen 1

PASSIVE *ep* The submissive, yielding nature is revealed in sprawling, formless strokes as are often observed in a final *s* with a lack of positiveness.

154

PATIENT *e* A person who can bear suffering or provocation with calmness and self-control may be either emotionally responsive or cool and collected. The writing will show self-control and an absence of irritability and temper. Generosity, broad-mindedness, and diplomatic ability are often in evidence.

PEACEFUL *e* Refer to "calm."

PECULIARITY *p* When an individual likes to be distinctive or different from the ordinary in some manner, he is said to have a peculiarity. This desire to be unique is revealed in circle formations used as dots for *i* and *j*. Even though the individual idiosyncrasy of the writer cannot be deduced, the fact that he has one can be.

The woman who wrote Specimen 2 couldn't bear to have her hair dressed in the same fashion worn by most women. She always wanted it to be different from the ordinary, even though the style was not becoming to her facial features.

Specimen 2

PEEVISH *p* An irritable person makes *i* and *j* dots with a jab stroke, resulting in irregular or arrow-like dashes instead of dots.

Specimen 3 was written by a woman whose children, husband, and housework irritated her so much that she was constantly peevish.

Specimen 3

PENETRATING *p* Showing keenness of mind. This type of mind is revealed in very sharp points on *m, n, r,* etc. The more needle-like the points, the keener is the comprehension.

Specimen 4

PENURIOUS *ep* Refer to "stingy."

PEPPERY *p* This means hot-tempered or irritable, and is determined by short, inflexible initial strokes or ricks, jabbed *i* and *j* dots, or pointed *t* bars that fall to the right of the *t* stem, particularly when pointed downward.

PEREMPTORY *e* Intolerantly positive. Such a person's writing shows extreme definiteness, narrow-mindedness, and often, domineering tendencies.

PERFECTIONIST *e* The person who strives for perfection goes back over his writing and corrects any missing

156

stroke or one made in error. Close attention to details is usually evident.

PERFIDIOUS *e* One who deliberately breaks faith, who is not trustworthy, is revealed in deliberate deceitfulness and lack of loyalty.

PERKY *e* A spirited, aggressive, or gay person's writing shows optimism, a sense of humor, and initiative or aggression.

PERMISSIVE *e* One who allows or consents to others' wishes is tolerant and lacks dominating or domineering tendencies; yielding strokes are often evident in his writing.

PERSEVERING, PERSEVERANCE

PERSISTENT, PERSISTENCE *p* These are synonyms describing the person who continues to do something in spite of difficulty or opposition, or the quality of so doing. Persistence carries the implication of steadfast or enduring perseverance, and is revealed in tied strokes (see Specimen 5) no matter where they are found in the writing.

Specimen 5

PERSONALITY. The definition of this variously defined noun most applicable from the standpoint of Grapho-analysis is "habitual patterns and qualities of behavior

157

of any individual as expressed by physical and mental activities and attitudes." Since handwriting is an expressive movement, mental habits and qualities can thereby be determined.

PERSPICACIOUS *ep* Having keen judgment or understanding. This is primarily determined by strong comprehensive ability and is enhanced by concentration and analytical ability. Comprehension is shown in sharp points on *m, n, h,* etc.; concentration is revealed in small writing; analytical ability is obvious when there are frequent *v* formations at the base line.

PERTINACIOUS *e* Holding firmly to some purpose, belief, or action, often stubbornly, is evidenced by frequent final hooks indicating strong tenacity and cross strokes or downstrokes that grow heavier at the end. The latter indicate increasingly strong will power when they go across, and increasingly great determination when they go down.

PESSIMISTIC *p* An individual who looks on the dark side of things and is always expecting the worst reveals this attitude in writing shown in Specimen 6 that slants downward, either single words or entire lines.

Specimen 6

PETTY *e* Tending to make much of small matters; narrow-minded. This is often revealed in sarcasm, irritability, analytical tendencies, sensitivity to criticism, and narrow-mindedness.

PETULANT *p* Refer to "peevish."

PHILANTHROPIC *e* Although this means generous, it carries an implication of interest in the general human welfare, and is applicable when the writing shows marked generosity plus philosophical or spiritual imagination and broad-mindedness.

159

PHILOSOPHIC *(AL) p* In Graphoanalysis this is used in reference to philosophical thinking or philosophical imagination, and is determined by large upper loops illustrated in Specimen 7.

Specimen 7

PHLEGMATIC *e* See "impassive."

PHRENETIC *e* Excessively excited, determined by extreme emotional reactions and disorganized strokes.

PHYSICAL MINDEDNESS *p* This is a Graphoanalytical term used to express a mental desire for physical activity. The person who possesses this attribute, even though physically unable to satisfy it, has a desire to use his body, his arms and legs, in some kind of sports or physical activity such as dancing. Specimen 8 shows that this trait is revealed in large *p* loops in lower case letters.

Specimen 8

PIQUANT *e* An interesting, stimulating personality is often characterized by a good sense of humor, wit, optimism, enthusiasm, and other qualities that are pleasing.

PITILESS *e* A person without sympathy for others reveals a cold nature with no generosity.

PLACID *e* Refer to "calm."

PLAIN-SPOKEN *p* The writer who speaks frankly makes small circle letters (see Specimen 9) such as *a, o, g,* etc., open at the top.

Specimen 9

POISE *ep* Emotional balance and stability are revealed in a vertical or near-vertical slant. This noun implies a lack of impulsiveness and a lack of extreme emotional expression.

Specimen 10

PONTIFICAL *e* This is often used to imply a haughty or arrogant dignity, in which case it is determined by a cool emotional nature with very tall, retraced *t* and *d* stems, often accompanied by domineering tendencies.

POOR-SPIRITED *e* A timorous nature is revealed when repression and self-consciousness are present with a lack of initiative, enthusiasm, and definiteness.

POSITIVE *p* Having the mind set or settled is determined by blunt or heavy finals.

Another meaning of this word is opinionated and it can be aptly applied with both definitions to the woman who wrote Specimen 11. Any opinion that she has is the right one; she is sure that she knows. Not only is she positive, she is also tenacious and clings to her ideas, as is evidenced in her frequent final hooks.

162

Specimen 11

POSSESSIVE *p* Characterized by a desire to own. This is determined by initial hooks, and can pertain both to tangibles and intangibles, to money or to love, etc. For an example of initial hooks, refer to Specimen 12 under "acquisitive."

POTENT *ep* Able to control or influence. Look for strong, heavy *t* crossings that indicate a dominating will and long ones showing enthusiasm.

POWERFUL *ep* Strong, influential. See "potent."

PRACTICAL *ep* Concerned with the application of knowledge to useful ends as opposed to the theoretical or speculative. Practical goal-setting is shown in *t* bars that do not fall above the *t* stems, as such high cross strokes represent a visionary purpose. Practical imagination is revealed in strong lower loops, illustrated in Specimen 12.

Specimen 12

PRAGMATICAL *e* Dogmatic; opinionated; conceited. This is revealed in a combination of positiveness, narrow-mindedness, and vanity. Look for blunt finals to strokes,

163

narrow, elongated, small circle letters, and extremely
high *t* and *d* stems.

PRECAUTIOUS *p* Refer to "caution," "cautious."

PRECIPITANT *e* Acting very hastily or rashly. This is
determined by high emotional reaction without restraining
influences such as self-control, caution, conservatism, etc.

PRECOCIOUS *e* When a child's mental development is more
advanced than is normal for his age group, it is revealed
in strokes showing keen comprehension and definiteness
of thinking.

PREJUDICED *ep* The individual who bases his opinions
on emotional reactions rather than cool judgment, writes
with a forward slant showing high to extreme emotional
reactiveness. This adjective may also be applied to the
writer with a more nearly vertical slant when his small
circle letters are narrow, as this reveals narrow-mindedness. In both cases, the writer forms opinions before all
the facts are known; in the first case, because of emotional
prejudices, in the second, because of preconceived ideas
and intolerance.
Specimen 13 shows both the extreme emotions and
narrow-mindedness.

Specimen 13

164

PREOCCUPIED *e* See "absent-minded."

PREPOSSESSED *ep* See "prejudiced."

PRESUMPTUOUS *e* When a person shows overconfidence, arrogance, or effrontery, his writing will have strokes showing the tendency to domineer, aggressiveness, and vanity.

PREVARICATE *p* One who evades the truth shows intentional deceit in his writing by making both initial and final loops inside his small circle letters. In some instances diplomatic ability leads to prevarication.

The student who wrote Specimen 14 managed to give many different excuses for not getting her work done, but never gave the true reason.

Specimen 14

PRIDE *p* This refers either to a justified or excessive belief in one's own worth, merit, superiority, etc., and when it is justified, it is considered an asset. The person who takes pride in his work does a better job than he would otherwise do; one who takes pride in his appearance naturally avoids slovenliness, etc. One who has pride sets a higher standard of conduct for himself than he would do without pride. It is when pride is excessive to the point of conceit or vanity that it becomes a liability.

Pride is determined by high *d* and *t* stems, either looped or retraced as indicated in Specimen 15. The degree to which one has pride is determined by the height of those stems in comparison to the rest of the writing.

thread made
should said

Specimen 15

PROCRASTINATION *ep* The habit of putting off doing something until a future time is revealed in *t* bars that fall to the left of the *t* stem and *i* and *j* dots that are made back of the *i* and *j*.

this jay to
is look th

Specimen 16

PRODIGAL *ep* An exceedingly or recklessly wasteful person, a spendthrift, lacks a good sense of values, and reveals this in extreme generosity and a complete lack of restraining traits such as conservatism and caution. Strong love of variety is usually present.

PROFESSIONAL. In order to be considered professional, a Graphoanalyst must strive to be worthy of the high standards set by Graphoanalysis.

PROFLIGATE *ep* Recklessly extravagant. Refer to "prodigal."

PROJECTION Psychologists and psychiatrists use this term to describe the process whereby an individual ascribes to others his own ideas or impulses, especially when such ideas or impulses are considered undesirable. Most Graphoanalytical counselors have the experience of hearing a counselee say, "But everybody else feels that way," or, "Most of the people I know do things like that," to justify his own behavioral traits. In such cases, quantitative rather than qualitative judgment on the part of the Graphoanalyst is important.

PROSAIC *e* Matter-of-fact; dull. This is determined by a lack of imagination, enthusiasm, and keen comprehension.

PROUD *p* Having or showing a proper pride in oneself, one's position, etc. Refer to "pride."

PROVIDENT *e* An economical person shows conservatism, practicality, and a lack of extravagance in his writing.

PRUDENT *e* This can mean either capable of exercising sound judgment in practical matters or cautious. In either case, conservatism will be present and the slant will not be extreme. Look for strokes indicating caution, attention to details, and lack of either extravagant generosity or imagination.

PRURIENT *e* Refer to "lustful."

PSYCHIC *e* When a person is apparently sensitive to forces beyond the physical world, frequent breaks between letter formations (intuitive ability) as shown in Specimen 17, and inflated upper loops (philosophical or spiritual thinking) are evident in his writing.

Specimen 17

PSYCHOPATHIC PERSONALITY   *e* The writing of such a person shows emotional instability (great variation in slant), lack of sound judgment (extravagance, intolerance, etc.), and impulsiveness. Amoral and asocial feelings and other serious personality defects characterize such a person.

PUERILE *e* The writing of a childish person shows that he is easily influenced, has not formed strong mental habits, lacks definiteness and emotional maturity.

PUGNACIOUS *e* One who is given to fighting or is quarrelsome shows resentment, aggressiveness, irritability, and temper. He is often overly sensitive to criticism.

PUNCTILIOUS *ep* Very exact. This is determined by dotting *i* and *j* close to the point (attention to details) and precise *t* crossings.

PUNCTUAL *ep* See "punctilious."

PUNGENT *e* When this is used figuratively it implies a penetrating or stimulating quality, and may be applied to a sense of humor when that trait is accompanied by sarcasm and keen comprehension. It may also be used to describe the trait of sarcasm when it is sharp and is also accompanied by keen comprehension or analytical ability.

PURPOSEFUL *ep* Having a purpose. This is shown in heavy crossbars for *t's,* which indicate a strong will (see Specimen 19). This word also means determined, in which case heavy downstrokes below the base line contribute to the purposefulness of the writer.

Specimen 19

PUSHING *ep* Refer to "aggressive."

Q

QUACK. A person who. with little or no foundation, pretends to have knowledge or skill in a particular field; charlatan. Any individual who represents himself as a certified Graphoanalyst and who has not so been certified by International Graphoanalysis Society, Inc., is a quack.

QUALITATIVE *versus* **QUANTITATIVE** in Graphoanalysis. One criterion of a scientific method of assessing personality traits is that it measures said traits. Handwriting analysis has been criticized by psychologists on the ground that many Graphoanalysts merely point out qualities (personal characteristics) of the writer that are common to everyone, instead of judging the quantity or the extent to which those qualities are present. A thorough training in Graphoanalysis enables one to assess personality traits quantitatively, to evaluate average, above average, and below average degrees of any one individual trait. In this respect, Graphoanalysis is more scientific than are some methods of handwriting analysis.

QUARRELSOME *e* One who is inclined to quarrel reveals this trait in his writing by showing a combination of resentment, irritability, talkativeness, and a desire to domineer.

QUIBBLER *e* One who evades the point by resorting to trivial faultfinding reveals in his writing analytical ability, some deceit, and irritability. Shallowness and resentment of imposition are often present.

QUICK *ep* Prompt to understand or learn. This can be applied to the writer's mind; one can deduce that he has a quick mind when *m's, n's, r's,* etc (see Specimen 1), are made with sharp points.

Specimen 1

QUIPSTER *ep* A person who makes witty or sarcastic allusions. Sarcasm is shown in arrow-like *t* crossbars. Wit is evaluated from a combination of light sarcasm and a sense of humor (initial flourishes that are not ostentatious).

QUIRK *ep* People who have a peculiar trait or mannerism show this primarily by use of circles instead of dots over *i's* and *j's*. This circle used as a dot is always evidence of a desire to be different from other people in some way, evidence of an idiosyncrasy.

It does not take very much study of Specimen 2 to conclude that the writer had a quirk that prevented him from being considered an average individual by his associates. Besides his desire to be different, his writing shows a combination of extreme vanity and extreme suppression of his intensely responsive emotional nature.

There should be freedom of publication.
writer he puts his best material forward
capable of doing a better job. A hien

QUITTER *e* A person who gives up easily without trying hard shows decreasing will power and decreasing determination by making crossbars and downstrokes that rapidly grow lighter after they are started.

QUIXOTIC *e* Idealistic; impractical; visionary. This is determined by a preponderance of large upper loops over lower ones and very high *t* bars.

R

RASH *e* Too hasty in acting or speaking. This is determined, as shown in Specimen 1, when the far forward slant shows the emotional responsiveness of the writer with no inhibiting influences such as conservatism, caution, etc. This type of person acts on impulse, without stopping to think of the consequences.

much for the informative
sent to me. I find it

RATIONAL *e* This implies the ability to reason logically and often connotes the absence of emotionalism. The writing of such a person shows no emotionalism in extreme slant; Specimen 2 illustrates the rounded *m's* and *n's* of the logical thinker.

Specimen 2

READY-WITTED *p* Quick in thought or understanding. A mentally quick writer makes sharp points on *m's, n's, r's,* and the lower part of *h's.* The more needle-like the points are, the faster he comprehends.

Specimen 3 is the writing of a student who was a challenge to her professors because of her ready wit.

Specimen 3

REALIST *ep* A person concerned with real things and practical matters rather than those that are imaginary or visionary shows stronger lower loops than upper loops and his *t* crossings do not fall above the *t* stems. Lower loops indicate thinking in the material realm; upper, in the theoretical or philosophical. *T* bars above the stem show visionary goal-setting; when they cross the stem--practical goal-setting.

The woman who wrote Specimen 4 was a realist. When her husband became ill she took the only kind of a job she could get, that of a waitress. She was not concerned about its not being a professional job with prestige, but rather she was concerned that the family would continue to have something to eat.

Specimen 4

RECKLESS *e* Refer to rash.

RELIABLE *e* When a person is dependable his writing will show a combination of loyalty, pride, persistence, and determination, with a lack of deceit, confusion of interests, and variability.

REPRESSED *ep* When an individual forces ideas and impulses that are painful to the conscious mind into his unconscious, it is revealed (see Specimen 5) in compressed or cramped strokes in his writing.

174

Specimen 5

RESENTMENT *p* People who are on the alert against imposition, who have a feeling of displeasure and indignation from a sense of being injured or offended, show this attribute as Specimen 6 illustrates in inflexible, initial strokes leading up to a letter from the base line, especially when such a straight stroke is not needed at the beginning of that letter.

Specimen 6

RESERVED *ep* Keeping one's thoughts and feelings to oneself. This is determined by narrow *e's, o's* and *a's* closed with a final loop (secrecy), and compression of strokes (repression). Self-consciousness and exclusiveness are frequently present, and the slant is usually near-vertical or vertical.

The student who wrote Specimen 7 had a difficult time making friends because of her extreme reserve.

175

With just the other members
own favorite dishes and
pride in preparing their
septem of the Utopian in
seem very practical or in

Specimen 7

RESIGNED *ep* Refer to "submissive."

RESILIENT *e* Recovering strength, spirits, good humor, etc., quickly. This trait is revealed in light line writing, a forward slant showing high or extreme emotional reactions, plus optimism (upward slant) and enthusiasm (long cross strokes).

RESOLUTE *e* The writing of one who has a fixed, firm purpose and determination is characterized by heavy *t* bars (strong purposes) and heavy down-strokes below the base line (determination). Persistence and tenacity are also present.

RESOURCEFUL *e* The person who can deal promptly and effectively with problems has marked analytical ability, definiteness of thinking, and initiative.

RESPONSIBILITY *p* An individual who wants responsibility has a desire for greater opportunity and is willing

176

to take on additional duties and obligations to gain it. This is evidenced by large initial circle loops (see Specimen 8), especially on capital letters.

Specimen 8

RESTLESS *p* When a person is always seeking change he reveals this by making large lower loops that often interfere with the strokes in the writing on the line below.

Specimen 9 was written by a man who has changed jobs numbers of times. No matter what job he held, he was active in other things such as amateur dramatics and community organizations—he was always on the go.

Specimen 9

177

RESTRAINED, RESTRAINT *ep* When anyone practices restraint, he suppresses or controls emotions and impulses. This is primarily determined by retraced, compressed strokes in *m* and *n* and generally squeezed writing. Self-control may be evident in bowed *t* bars when both ends of the bar are lower than the center.

RETICENT *ep* Refer to "reserved".

RETIRING *ep* One who draws back from contact with others writes with a vertical or backhand slant. Exclusiveness and reserve usually are evident.

Note the slant and the marked clannishness in Specimen 10.

Specimen 10

RHYTHM *p* When the movement of the pen is characterized by basically regular recurrence of beat, the written strokes illustrated in Specimen 11 return to the base line with an even spacing between stroke combinations.

Specimen 11

RIGID *e* One who is unyielding can be determined when the writing shows definiteness of thinking and a lack of yielding strokes. Stubbornness, loyalty to ideals, and narrow-mindedness are frequently evident.

RUDE *e* Discourteous. The word implies a deliberate lack of consideration for others' feelings, and is applicable when the writing shows bluntness and self-interest. Ostentation, vanity, and talkativeness are often evident.

RUFFLES *p* When a person is easily irritated or annoyed it is revealed in his writing by jab strokes for dot over *i* and *j*.

Specimen 12

RUTHLESS *e* Refer to "pitiless."

179

S

SAGACIOUS *p* One who is keenly perceptive or discerning makes sharp points on *m, n, r,* etc. The more needle-like the points are, the greater is the writer's sagacity. See specimens under "comprehension."

SALACIOUS *e* Refer to "lustful."

SANGUINE *p* An optimistic person writes with an upward slant to lines or words. This characteristic is also indicated in final strokes and cross strokes that slant upward.
  This man's sanguine temperament, shown in Specimen 1 is revealed primarily in his upward slanting *t* bars.

Specimen 1

SARCASTIC *p* A person who is characterized by cutting or caustic remarks makes knife-blade cross strokes--see Specimen 2. The heavier the stroke, the more biting is the sarcasm.

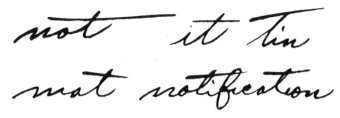

SARDONIC, SATIRICAL *p* These are synonyms of "sarcastic."

SAVING *ep* An economical individual is determined by evidence of conservatism: the writing is compressed with narrow spaces between letter formations (see Specimen 3) and *d* and *t* stems are often retraced.

Specimen 3

SCATTER-BRAINED *e* A flighty, frivolous person is revealed when the writing shows confusion of interests and a lack of definiteness. Shallowness and a vivid imagination may also be evident.

SCHOLARLY *e* The individual who has much knowledge, accuracy, and critical ability will show in his writing strong investigative and analytical ability, a good memory, and, usually, philosophical thinking. Upper loops will be pointed rather than rounded.

SCIENTIFIC *ep* When a person has the type of mind that observes, studies, and systematizes facts his *m's, n's,* and *r's* have broad-topped but well defined stroke combinations indicated in Specimen 4. This ability is enhanced when the writer also possesses analytical ability and a good memory.

Specimen 4

SCOLD *e* One who angrily finds fault with others and nags reveals irritability (jab strokes for dots over *i* and *j*), talkativeness (open-mouthed circle letters), and resentment (inflexible initial strokes leading up from the base line to a letter).

SCRIMPY *ep* Refer to "stingy."

SCRUPULOUS *e* Careful attention to what is proper is revealed in careful dotting of *i's* and *j's*, careful crossing of *t's*, and retraced *t* and *d* stems (see Specimen 5). Loyalty to ideals and lack of deceit will also be evident, as the scrupulous person is conscientiously honest.

182

*Another good arguement
vith education through boo
ading itself is education
ooks and know good, but
he other books to know*

SECLUSIVE *ep* One who withdraws from association with others is primarily shown in Specimen 6--tiny round or squared loops on *y, g,* and *j* that indicate clannishness. Timidity is often present, and the slant usually is vertical or backhand rather than far forward.

*astronomy, agriculture, music
Milton says, which struck
he has time during some*

SECRETIVE *p* Tending to conceal one's thoughts, feelings, affairs, etc. from others; not frank or open. This is determined by small circle letters as *a, o,* and *g* that are closed with a final loop (see Specimen 7). Narrow or closed *e's* are also indicative of this trait.

ormond error
gore grove

SECTARIAN *ep* Refer to "narrow-minded."

SEDATE *e* A calm, dignified person writes with a near-vertical or vertical slant and makes tall, retraced *t* and *d* stems. The connotation of serious for this word involves a lack of frivolity and humor.

SEDULOUS *e* One who is diligent and persistent shows determination, will power, and strong persistence in his writing. Determination is shown by heavy, long down-strokes below the base line; will power by heavy *t* crossings; persistence by tie strokes which may occur in many different letters.

SELECTIVE *p* One who is careful in choosing or selecting friends reveals this by making narrow lower loops, particularly on *g, y,* and *j.*

many give may
theory duty

184

SELF-ASSERTIVE *e* A forward, pushing, person shows initiative and/or aggressiveness and a dominating or domineering will power.

SELF-ASSURANCE *p* Refer to "self-reliance."

SELF-CENTERED *e* An egocentric, selfish person writes with a vertical or backhand slant, compressed strokes, lack of generosity. Vanity is frequently present.

SELF-CONFIDENCE *p* See "self-reliance."

SELF-CONSCIOUS *p* The person who is unduly conscious of himself as an object of notice, who is shy and ill-at-ease in the presence of others, reveals this characteristic in Specimen 9 by making his final stroke on *m* and *n* higher than the rest of the letter.

Specimen 9

SELF-CONTAINED *ep* One meaning of this is showing self-command, and is determined primarily by bowed cross strokes.

In the above sense it may well be applied to the writer of Specimen 10. Although only one of the three *t's* in this sample has a bow crossing, the stroke appears frequently enough in his writing to justify the conclusion that he uses his will power for self-control. This writing was done with the feet of a male college student who has no hands; it is not handwriting, but it is writing directed by the brain, as is all writing.

Specimen 10

SELF-CONTROL *p* Control of one's emotions, desires, actions, etc. This is determined by *t* crossbars that are bowed upward (see Specimen 11), with both ends of the bar turned down from the center.

Specimen 11

SELF-DECEIT *p* The person who acts on half-impressions (which are really false impressions) as if they were the truth is actually deceiving himself. This attribute is shown in Specimen 12 in an initial loop inside small circle letters such as *a, o, g,* etc.

186

Specimen 12

SELF-ESTEEM *p* This can mean either self-respect or undue pride in oneself. In case of the former, dignity and pride will be evident in tall, retraced *d* and *t* stems. If the latter meaning is used, pride to the point of vanity is shown in *t* and *d* stems that are so tall that they are at least three times as high as the small circle letters, and they may be either retraced or looped.

SELF-IMPORTANT *p* Having an exaggerated opinion of one's own importance is evident when *t*'s and *d*'s are extremely tall as in Specimen 13. They may be made either with a stem or a loop.

Specimen 13

187

SELFISH *ep* The individual who has so much regard for his own interests that the welfare of others is of little concern to him shows self-interest by writing with a near-vertical slant and compressed strokes (see Specimen 14). There will be an absence of long finals indicating generosity in such a person's writing.

Specimen 14

SELF-POSSESSED *ep* The calm, composed writer has a near-vertical slant showing poise and cool judgment, and an absence of jabbed strokes showing irritability and temper.

SELF-RELIANCE, SELF-RELIANT *p* One who has confidence in his own abilities is determined when the writer makes strong underscores in signatures or other writing.

Specimen 15

188

SELF-RESTRAINT *p* One who possesses this trait makes a conscious effort to control his behavior, to overcome some habit or characteristic that he considers to be a weakness. As Specimen 16 shows it is determined by *t* crossbars that are turned upward in the center.

Specimen 16

SELF-SUFFICIENT *ep* When this means independent it is revealed in very short *t* and *d* stems, and is often accompanied by the small squared or circled lower loops that indicate clannishness.

SELF-WILLED *p* Refer to "stubborn."

SENILITY *e* This is a condition of old age resulting in weakness of mind and body. When the neural impulses are weakened, the writing of the individual becomes shaky, disorganized, and, often, corrugated. Since this happens to younger people when they are afflicted with certain diseases, the Graphoanalyst cannot pinpoint the cause of the shaky appearance of the writing without some prior knowledge of the writer.

Specimen 17 was written by a woman who was in her eighties at the time. It took a great deal of effort for her to write so that the words were legible.

189

Specimen 17

SENSITIVE *p* The meaning of this word as it is used in Graphoanalysis is limited to easily offended, disturbed, shocked, or hurt by the actions of others, and is used in conjunction with the word criticism, i.e., sensitive to criticism. The trait is determined by looped *d's* and *t's* shown in Specimen 18. The more inflated the loops are, the higher degree of sensitivity the writer has.

Specimen 18

SENSUAL, SENSUALITY *p* Preoccupied with bodily or sexual pleasures. This implies excessive indulgence in gross sensual pleasures, and is revealed in what is called in Graphoanalysis, "muddy writing." It is heavy writing (see Specimen 19) with heavy blots and corrugations on the strokes.

190

Specimen 19

SENSUOUS, SENSUOUSNESS *p* This suggests the strong appeal of that which is pleasing to the eye, ear, touch, etc., and implies susceptibility to the pleasures of sensation. It is determined by strong, heavy, strokes illustrated in Specimen 20. The strokes will be clean-cut with few, if any, blots and no corrugations on the strokes.

Specimen 20

SERVILE *e* The humbly yielding or submissive writer shows many yielding strokes with a lack of definiteness and pride.

SEVERE *e* This applies to a person who is strict and un-compromising; it connotes a total absence of softness, laxity, frivolity, etc. The writing will show definiteness, loyalty to ideas and ideals, self-interest, and reserve. It will lack generosity, humor, and ostentation.

SEX. Whether or not a writer is male or female cannot be definitely determined by handwriting.

SEXUALITY *e* A highly developed interest in and concern with sex, when the sexual appetite is above normal, is determined by heavy writing that is frequently badly blotted with clogged circle or loop strokes and corrugated edges.

SHALLOW *ep* Lacking depth of character, intellect, or meaning; superficial. This is revealed in basin-like *t* cross-ings and shallow points on *m, n,* etc.

Specimen 21

SHIFTLESS *e* Lacking the will or ability to do or accom-plish. Look for weak will power and determination, very low-placed goals, indefiniteness, no enthusiasm, energy, or initiative.

SHIFTY *e* An evasive person's writing will show deceit, indefiniteness, variability, and lack of loyalty.

SHORT-TEMPERED *e* When an individual has a tendency to lose his temper easily, the writing will have initial short, inflexible, tick strokes without the restraining influence of self-restraint. Numerous jab strokes showing high irritability are usually present.

SHOWMANSHIP *ep* Skill in presenting anything in an interesting or dramatic manner, based on a desire to attract favorable attention to oneself, is revealed in large writing with well-made flourishes and unusually large, well-formed signatures (see Specimen 22). This is frequently coupled with self-reliance.

Specimen 22

SHREWD *e* This implies keenness of mind, sharp insight, and cleverness in practical matters. It is determined by keen comprehension and analytical ability plus practical imagination. Some deceit may be present.

SHREWISH *e* A disposition to nag and to have an evil temper is revealed in irritability and temper plus talkativeness, analytical ability, and, frequently, sarcasm.

SHY *e* Timid: extremely self-conscious. Self-consciousness and inhibitions will be obvious in the writing of such a person, as evidenced in final humps of *m* and *n* that are higher than the rest of the letter and in retraced and compressed strokes. Aggressiveness and self-reliance are usually absent.

SIMPLICITY *e* When a person prefers plainness or naturalness to elegance and luxury, his strokes will not be excessively heavy and will be made without flourishes indicating ostentation. When the writer desires simplicity and directness rather than affectation or subtlety, many letters that usually start with a loop, such as *b, f, t,* will be made with a single downstroke instead of the loop.

SINCERE *e* This implies an absence of deceit or hypocrisy and an adherence to the simple truth. The characteristic is determined by loyalty to that which the individual thinks is right (revealed in small round dots for *i* and *j*) and an absence of deceit (double-looped small circle letters indicate deceit). Diplomatic ability may be indicated, but it will not be marked.

SKEPTICAL *ep* A doubting, questioning individual will not accept religious doctrines or other matters that are generally accepted without investigating and analyzing them on his own. This characteristic is primarily shown in analytical ability and an inquiring type of mind. Independence of thought, resentment, and irritability frequently are present, but there will be no yielding strokes (see Specimen 23) that indicate the writer is easily influenced by others.

Specimen 23

SLAVISH *e* Refer to servile.

SLOTH *e* A disinclination to exert oneself is revealed in very low-placed goals (low *t* crossings), slow, deliberate strokes, an absence of initiative or energetic, forward-moving strokes.

SLY *e* A secretive or wily nature is revealed in final loops closing small circle letters (secretiveness) and double (both initial and final) loops closing the same kind of letters (deceitfulness) coupled with fairly sharp comprehension.

SMALL-MINDED *e* The writing of a narrow, petty, selfish person shows self-interest, narrow-mindedness, selfishness, and, often, resentment.

SOCIABLE *e* A friendly person who enjoys the company of others shows some emotional responsiveness and is not reticent, timid, or highly self-conscious. Mental alert-

195

ness is often indicated.

SPENDTHRIFT *e* Such a person is extravagant and lacks a good sense of values. This is determined by excessive generosity with an absence of conservatism and caution. Extreme love of change and variety is often present.

SPIRITED *e* This adjective may be applied to the disposition of the writer whose strokes show mental vigor and energy. There will be a forceful forward sweep to the strokes; enthusiasm and mental alertness will be evident.

SPITEFUL *e* The writing of a person who purposefully hurts others will be full of resentment and biting sarcasm, often showing impulsiveness.

SPONTANEOUS *ep* The person who acts on impulse is revealed when the slant of the writing is forward and there are no or very few indications of inhibiting traits (see Specimen 24). An extremely emotionally responsive person shows spontaneity at times, even when inhibited.

Specimen 24

STABILITY *e* In Graphoanalysis this is most commonly used to refer to emotional stability, in which case the slant of the writing is neither extreme nor variable to any great degree. If used to mean firmness of purpose, *t* crossings will be heavy in comparison to the other strokes in the writing.

STIFF *ep* When used to mean constrained, the writer's strokes will be compressed, showing repression. With a nearly vertical or vertical slant the writing will show the writer's lack of emotional expressiveness. If the word is used to mean stubborn, wigwam-like strokes will be evident, coupled with the blunt finals that show positiveness.

STINGY *ep* This implies a grudging reluctance to part with anything belonging to one, and is revealed in compressed writing, shown in Specimen 25, with no generosity and few open circle formations.

Specimen 25

STOLID *e* Having or showing little or no emotion. This is determined when the writing is near-vertical or vertical and the strokes are light or, if they are heavy, repression of emotions is obvious.

STRAIGHTFORWARD *p* A frank individual is determined by small circle letters (see Specimen 26), *a, o, g*, etc., that are open at the top and *e's* made as a circle.

197

frank and outspoken

Specimen 26

STUBBORN *p* One who is unreasonably determined to have his own way, refusing to yield even in the face of facts, is revealed by stroke combinations that form a wigwam, illustrated in Specimen 27. This formation is most often noted in *d* and *t*, but it retains the same significance no matter where it appears.

rat m did

Specimen 27

STUPID *e* When a person lacks normal intelligence his writing will show lack of comprehension, analytical ability, fluidity of thinking, etc.

SUBMISSIVE *ep* A yielding nature is revealed in yielding strokes, as in rounded, unformed small *s's*, coupled with a lack of dominating or stubborn tendencies.

SUBTLE *ep* One meaning of this is keen, penetrating. It may be applied to the mind of the writer when his strokes show keen comprehension; to his sense of humor when both humor and keen comprehension are present, etc.

SULKY, SULLEN *e* These both have connotations of resentment and ill-humor coupled with withdrawal. When resentment strokes and irritability are prominent in writing that shows an inhibited nature, and there are frequent strokes made from right to left to indicate withdrawal, these adjectives may well be used to describe the writer.

SUPERCILIOUS *e* Refer to "arrogant."

SUPERFICIAL *ep* This implies concern with only the obvious or surface aspects of a thing and is a synonym of "shallow." It is determined by basin-like *t* bars and very short or shallow points as in *m* and *n* (see Specimen 28). Attention to details and desire for responsibility will be absent.

Specimen 28

SUPERIORITY COMPLEX *e* A feeling of superiority, often accompanied by excessive aggressiveness and a domineering attitude, is likely to be a compensation for feelings of inferiority. Look for vanity, aggressiveness, and domineering tendencies. Ostentation is frequently in evidence.

SUPPRESSED *p* When ideas, desires, or feelings are deliberately excluded from consciousness or overt action, the individual is considered suppressed. This is determined by compressed writing in Specimen 29 and narrow

199

spaces between letter formations.

Specimen 29

SUSCEPTIBLE *p* Easily affected emotionally; responsive. This is determined by the forward slant of the upstrokes of the writing. The farther they slant to the right on the emotional gauge, the more susceptible is the writer.

SUSPICIOUS *ep* Tending habitually to suspect, especially to suspect fault, evil, etc. This tendency shown in Specimen 30 is primarily revealed in a highly developed analytical sense (frequent v formations at the base line), usually coupled with resentment (inflexible initial strokes). A well developed imagination is often indicated.

Specimen 30

SYMPATHETIC *ep* When one has the nature to feel pity or compassion for others' suffering, when one is able to enter into others' feelings and emotions, he is said to have a sympathetic nature. This is primarily revealed in a forward slant, showing the writer's emotional responsiveness, and is accompanied by generosity and an absence of negative traits.

SYSTEMATIC *p* Refer to "orderly."

200

T

TACITURN *p* An uncommunicative person closes his small circle letters such as *a* and *o* with a final loop inside the circle (see Specimen 1) or makes narrow, closed *e's* and other circle letters.

Specimen 1

TACTFUL *p* Refer to "diplomatic."

TALENT, TALENTED *ep* This implies having a native ability for a specific pursuit and connotes either that it is or can be cultivated by the one possessing it. Some of the basic indications of talent are listed below, but evaluation must be used to arrive at a conclusion as to the ability of the writer to cultivate the talent.

ARTISTIC Good sense of color (heavy writing), good sense of line values (graceful lines), creative ability (broad or square-topped *m's, n's,* and *r's*).

LITERARY Fluidity of thought (smoothly reversed lower *f* loops, figure-eight *g's*), desire for culture (Greek *e's*), and delta *d's*. Good comprehension is important.

POETIC Fluidity of thought, good sense of rhythm (equal spaces between letter formations), good imagination, particularly in philosophical areas.

SCIENTIFIC Investigative type of thinker, strong analytical ability, ability to concentrate.

201

Space does not allow a complete list here of indications of talent.

Study of the general and graduate courses in Graphoanalysis is necessary in order to gain such knowledge.

TALKATIVE *p* One who is fond of talking leaves many of his small circle letters such as *a, o, d,* and *g* open at the top.

In spite of being a reserved person, the writer of Specimen 2 is extremely talkative when he is with friends or acquaintances.

Specimen 2

TATTLER *e* One who gossips. Refer to "gossipy."

TEMPER *p* When this is used to indicate the trait of having a tendency to become angry readily it is revealed by inflexible strokes (see Specimen 3) that are short, or made as ticks, at the beginning of a group of strokes.

Specimen 3

TEMPERAMENTAL *e* The person with an excitable temperament, who is easily upset, has a far forward slant, showing that he is highly emotionally reactive, without its being accompanied by controlling influences such as conservatism or self-control.

Many artists (other people, too) have temperament because they have dispositions that rebel at restraint and are often moody or capricious. Variability of slant and ostentation are often evident in the writing of such people.

TEMPERATE *e* The writing of one who is moderate in indulging the appetites shows either a lack of sensuousness or sensuality (light line or only moderately heavy strokes) or, if the writing is heavy, it will be accompanied by self-restraint.

TEMPESTUOUS *e* A turbulent nature is revealed by extreme emotional expression accompanied by marked irritability or temper and resentment.

TENACIOUS *p* When a person holds firmly, or clings to whatever he owns and to whatever he believes (his ideas and ideals), he reveals this by making final hooks to his strokes (see Specimen 4). The hooks, large or small, may be found at the end of a cross stroke or a

203

downstroke. The smaller his hooks, the more tenacious he is in small matters. However, final hooks should not be confused with final flourishes.

Specimen 4

TENACITY *p* In Graphoanalysis, when this is used in the meaning of the quality of being tenacious, it is determined by final hooks. When the meaning of persistence is applied, it is determined by tie strokes.

TESTY *p* See "irritable."

THOROUGH *ep* One who is very exact, especially with regard to details, shows close attention to details by dotting *i*'s and *j*'s close to their points. Precision is shown in the crossing of *t*'s and other stroke formations in general. Persistence, tenacity, and determination are often evident.

THOUGHTLESS *ep* Refer to "impetuous."

THRIFTY *e* An economical person writes with narrow spaces between strokes and combinations of strokes. There will be no signs of extravagance in long finals and inflated imagination loops.

Being thrifty does not rule out generosity, but rather it implies care in management of one's resources. The writer of Specimen 5 is not without generosity. She does have to manage her expenditures very carefully in order to make a successful wife to a man with a limited income.

ton uses. He feels that the
to determine the right book
ilton believes that people wi
t that they are now having

Specimen 5

TIMID *e* Lacking self-confidence; shy. Reserve will be marked and self-consciousness and clannishness are frequently indicated in the writing of a timid person.

TOLERANT *ep* Inclined to tolerate others' beliefs and practices. This is determined primarily by broad-mindedness and is more often found in the person who is not deeply emotional. Vanity and resentment will not be present.

TORPID *e* Dull; apathetic. The writing will show a lack of comprehension, initiative, and purpose.

TOUCHY *e* An easily offended writer shows sensitivity to criticism in looped *t* and *d* stems, resentment in inflexible initial strokes going up from the base line to a stroke combination, irritability in jabbed dots over *i* and *j*. Temper and pride may also be noted.

TRACTABLE *e* When a person is easily controlled his writing will show submissiveness and indefiniteness (see Specimen 6) with a lack of temper, stubbornness, independence of thinking, and strong will power.

Specimen 6

TRAIT A distinguishing quality or characteristic, especially of personality. No trait is unique to any one individual; it may be predominant in the writing of many persons. The uniqueness of each personality lies in the particular degree to which the individual possesses all his characteristics; it lies in the overall pattern of his traits.

TRANQUIL *e* A calm, placid individual's writing will show neither a variable nor a highly expressive emotional nature. It will lack irritability, temper, resentment, etc.

TRAVEL (DESIRE FOR) *p* This is shown in the long lower loops that reveal a love of change and variety. Such writers like to go from one place to another, are bored with a sedentary life.

This seventy-year-old woman's handwriting, Specimen 7, shows that her desire for travel is just as keen as it was when she was a young woman.

206

TRICKY *p* Refer to "deceitful."

TRIFLER *ep* One who treats without earnestness, full attention, or definite purpose, persons or ideas reveals this characteristic in shallowness with a lack of strong purpose or keen comprehension.

TRUTHFUL *e* An honest person's writing shows loyalty to his ideals in small round dots for *i*'s and *j*'s and a lack of double-looped small circle letters that show deceit. Uncontrolled imagination and talkativeness, which are conducive to uncontrolled statements, will not be in evidence.

TURBULENT *e* Disturbed, agitated. This is revealed by the far forward slant showing intense emotional responsiveness combined with aggressiveness and resentment.

TYRANNICAL *ep* An arbitrary, despotic individual is primarily determined by arrow-like *t* bars that are written from left to right and slant downward illustrated in Specimen 8. Vanity, resentment, and narrowmindedness often accompany this desire to domineer over others.

Specimen 8

U

ULTRACONSERVATIVE *ep* Conservative to an extreme degree is evaluated from the primary trait of conservatism when the compressed writing and retraced strokes are much more consistently present in the writing of one person than in that of the general population.

UMBRAGEOUS *e* When the writer is easily offended or aroused to suspicion his strokes will show resentment (initial inflexible strokes from the base line to a letter), strong sensitivity to criticism (inflated *t* and *d* stems), analytical ability (*v* formations at the base line) and, frequently, irritability or temper.

UNASSUMING *e* When a person is modest, not forward, his writing will show no ostentation, only moderate pride, and no aggressiveness. Inhibitions and self-consciousness are often present.

Specimen 1 is the writing of an unassuming young man who, though a good mechanic, had no pretensions of being other than an ordinary workman.

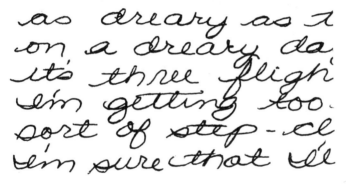

Specimen 1

UNBALANCED *e* An unstable person's writing shows variability, lack of organization (balance between upper and lower loops), and lack of rhythm. Certain individual traits may be exaggerated.

UNCERTAIN *p* Vague; not definite or determined. This is revealed in weak finals.

In a complete page of writing, the author of Specimen 2 had not a single blunt final. Alcoholism and uncertainty in his home life background may have been contributing factors in his lack of a definite mental approach to life.

Specimen 2

UNCONCERNED *e* See "indifferent."

UNDEMONSTRATIVE *ep* Giving little outward expression of the feelings is primarily determined by writing that does not slant very far to the right, but this adjective may also be applied to the writer with an emotionally expressive nature who is reserved. The writing may have a forward slant, but expressiveness is held in check when secretiveness and repression are present.

There are some variations in the slant of the upstrokes in Specimen 3, as there are in most handwriting, but the slant shows a cool, poised nature consistently enough that one may know that the writer is undemonstrative.

210

of learning theories
education courses, th
interesting to me. a
made it more intere
a vital part of moder

Specimen 3

UNDERSTANDING *e* A person characterized by comprehension and sympathy displays these traits in his writing. Comprehension is revealed in points on *m, n, r,* etc.; a sympathetic nature is shown in a forward slant that may indicate either a poised or a highly emotionally responsive person, with a lack of negative qualities such as vanity, the tendency to domineer, etc.

UNSELFISH *ep* Opposite of selfish. The individual who is willing to share his time and energy or his belongings with others reveals this by making long finals and wide spaces between stroke combinations.

The young woman who wrote Specimen 4 was always more willing to spend money on others' needs than on her own.

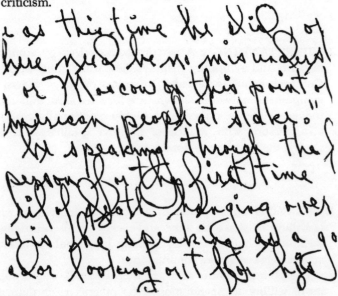

He said that publication could long as it was

Specimen 4

UNSETTLED *e* One who is not settled shows restlessness and confusion in his writing.

This man's unsettled condition seen in Specimen 5 is revealed not only in his confusion of interests and inflated, sometimes undirected, imagination, but also in the insecurity shown in his extremely prominent sensitivity to criticism.

Specimen 5

212

UNSTABLE *ep* One meaning of this is emotionally unsettled or variable, and may be applied to the writer who
writes with slant that varies considerably. Strokes may
be partly backhand and partly forward-slanting. Other
indications of instability are found when desire for change
and variety is extreme. See Specimen 5.

Note the extreme variations in slant in Specimen 6.

Specimen 6

V

VACILLATING *ep* One who is indecisive, irresolute, lacks
a definite mental approach to life. This is shown primarily
in weak final strokes (see Specimen 1). The writer's will
power or sense of purpose will not be strong (*t* crossings
are either light or rapidly grow lighter if the *t* bar starts
heavy).

213

Specimen 1

VACUOUS *e* Having lack of intelligence, interest, or thought. The writing of such a person will show a weak sense of purpose and either a lack of comprehension or shallowness.

VAGUE *e* Not sharp, certain, or precise in thought or expression. Look for indefiniteness of thinking and lack of rhythm and precision in the writing.

VAIN *ep* A conceited person has an excessively high regard for himself—his ability, looks, possessions, etc. This is primarily determined by exceedingly high *d* and *t* stems shown in Specimen 2. Selfishness and ostentation may be evident.

Specimen 2

214

VANITY *ep* The quality of being vain.

VAPID *e* Uninteresting; lifeless; dull; unexciting. People reveal this characteristic in handwriting when there is a lack of enthusiasm, definiteness of thinking, wit or humor, comprehension, emotional expressiveness, and other stimulating traits.

VARIABLE *ep* A changeable nature is primarily determined when the writing has a variable slant: strokes are made with a forward slant, then vertical or backhand. Strong desire for variety to the point of a confusion of interests may account for one's being considered variable. This is shown in long upper and lower loops illustrated in Specimen 3 that extend into lines of writing above and below.

Specimen 3

VARIETY (DESIRE FOR) *p* The individual who does not like monotony or sameness shows his desire for variety in long loops. The longer the loops are in comparison to the rest of the writing, the greater is his desire for change.

The man who wrote Specimen 4 would never be happy in a routine job. He is the manager of a credit union and, as such, has many and varied duties to perform. Note the length of his *y* loops.

Payments on this

be due monthly and

Check or money orde

Specimen 4

VEHEMENT *p* Characterized by intense feeling or passionate expression. One whose actions or movements are so characterized writes with a forward slant showing strong to intense emotional reactions (see Specimen 5). Strokes will be fairly heavy to very heavy.

nd so far you

nd so farm

Specimen 5

VENAL *e* The writing of a mercenary person who can readily be bribed or corrupted will show strong acquisitiveness, deceit, and a lack of loyalty and philosophical thinking.

216

VENGEFUL *e* The emotionalism of a vindictive person may be either expressed or repressed, but it will be deep. Resentment, marked irritability, sarcasm, and the tendency to domineer may be present.

VERACIOUS *e* The habitually truthful or accurate person will show very little or no self-deceit and no intentional deceit in his writing. Attention to details and loyalty to ideals are frequently present.

VERSATILE *ep* One who is competent in many things, who is capable of turning easily from one subject or occupation to another, is determined primarily by the penetrating points on *m*, *n*, and *r* that show a fast thinker (see Specimen 6). Fluidity of thought is often present. Limiting qualities such as self-consciousness and repression will be absent.

Specimen 6

VIBRANT *e* The writing of a vigorous, energetic person shows a strong forward sweep. Enthusiasm (long *t* bars) is usually prominent. The vigor and energy of the writer are those of the mind, not of the body, as the latter quality does not show in handwriting.

VIGOROUS *e* Acting with energy and force. This may be applied to the mind of the writer who shows good comprehension, a strong sense of purpose, strong determination, and definiteness.

VINDICTIVE *e* Refer to "vengeful."

VIOLENT *ep* Showing, or resulting from, strong feeling or emotion. This characteristic is revealed in a far forward slant with moderate to heavy strokes, showing the intense emotional reaction of the writer. When used to refer to temper, tick strokes, jab dots, and downward slanting, arrow-like *t* bars will be very heavy.

VISIONARY *p* A person who is characterized by impractical ideas or schemes builds air castles instead of setting his goals at an attainable level. He makes light *t* bars, see Specimen 7, that fall above the tops of the *t* stems. These strokes may be either short or long. When they are long, they reveal the writer's inner enthusiasm for his dream castle.

Specimen 7

VITALITY *e* Mental or physical vigor. The latter cannot be deduced from writing, but mental vigor is revealed in sharp comprehension and a powerful forward sweep to the strokes.

VITRIOLIC *p* Refer to "sarcastic."

VITUPERATIVE *e* One who is characterized by bitter, abusive language shows sarcasm, resentment, and talkativeness in his writing. Sarcasm is revealed by arrow-like *t* crossings; resentment by initial inflexible strokes leading up from the base line to a letter; talkativeness by openmouthed circle letters.

VIXENISH *e* See "shrewish."

VOLATILE *ep* A changeable nature is revealed in a slant that varies more than normal. However, any extremely emotionally reactive person will have volatile moods because he responds so readily to emotional situations.

When anyone's slant is as far to the right as the slant of Specimen 8, one can safely conclude that the writer has a volatile nature.

Specimen 8

VOLCANIC *e* Violently and powerfully explosive or capable of explosion. It is always a danger signal when handwriting shows a person who is inexpressive and highly repressed, yet who has very deep feelings. Such a person may explode, figuratively speaking, when his self-restraint reaches a breaking point.

VOLUBLE *ep* The person who is characterized by a great flow of words leaves small circle letters such as *a, o,* and *g* open at the top. Fluency of thought and speech is often evident.

It would be difficult to get a word in edgewise around the woman who wrote Specimen 9. Her fluidity of speech is shown in her *f*'s; her talkativeness in her open *a*'s, *o*'s, and *g*'s. No subject can be mentioned about which she does not have an opinion, which opinion she reveals at great length.

Specimen 9

VOLUPTUOUS *p* Refer to "sensual."

VORACIOUS *ep* Very greedy or eager in some desire or pursuit. This is shown in an excessive number of initial hooks, showing acquisitiveness to the point of greed. However, in the case of "muddy" writing, one might say the writer has a voracious desire for sensual pleasures.

VULGAR *ep* When one is characterized by a lack of culture, refinement, and sensitivity, the writing often shows sensuality or ostentation with an absence of the desire for culture or the desire to conform to socially acceptable standards of conduct.

VULNERABLE *p* An easily wounded person shows his sensitivity to criticism in large *t* and *d* loops.

Even though the writer of Specimen 10 is a very poised person, his vulnerability is revealed in his *t* and *d* loops.

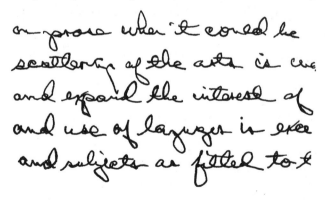

Specimen 10

W

WARMHEARTED *e* A kind, sympathetic person's writing shows an emotionally responsive nature and generosity without harsh qualities such as the tendency to domineer, sarcasm, resentment, etc.

WARY *p* A cautious writer fills in spaces at the end of the line with long final strokes.

The final strokes at the ends of the lines in Specimen 1 are not unusually long, but they are very significant. In a complete page of script, the writer had no long finals except those found at the ends of lines, thus clearly indicating his wary outlook.

Specimen 1

WASTEFUL *e* See "extravagant."

WILL *p* In Graphoanalysis the meaning used for this is "purpose," and it is determined by the weight, or width, of *t* bars in comparison to the rest of the writing strokes (see Specimen 2). The heavier the *t* bar, the stronger purpose has the writer.

WILLFUL *ep* When one follows his own will unreason-
ingly he is inclined to domineer over others.

Note the heaviness of the following *t* bars in Specimen
3 with their tendency to slant downward.

WINDY *e* One who talks much and says little is revealed
in a combination of talkativeness and shallowness. An
inflated imagination may be indicated.

WISHY-WASHY *e* A weak character is indicated by indefiniteness of thinking combined with submissiveness.
The writing will have no evidences of strong purpose or
determination.

WITHDRAWN *p* Withdrawing within oneself is indicated
when strokes are made from right to left, particularly
noticeable in final strokes. For other interpretations of
withdrawn, refer to "shy" and "reserved."

Although outwardly socially successful in college, the
young man who wrote Specimen 4 reveals his habit of

withdrawing from family and associates in his *f* and *y* final strokes.

Specimen 4

WITTY *ep* A synonym of this is humorous, but witty implies a sharp cleverness, sometimes with sarcasm. A good sense of humor is indicated by initial flourishes that are not ostentatious. When combined with light sarcasm (arrow-like cross strokes), witty is the more applicable trait designation.

WOOLGATHERING *p* The habit of daydreaming or indulging in fancies is revealed in light *t* bars made above the *t* stems.

Specimen 5

WORDY *e* This implies the use of more words than are necessary for communication. Look for extreme frankness, possibly accompanied by a vivid imagination and lack of poise and self-control.

224

WRONGHEADED *p* Stubbornly refusing to yield or agree, even when wrong. Refer to Specimen 27 under "stubborn."

Y

YIELDING *ep* A submissive nature is revealed in strokes that lack definiteness. This is often noticeable in a sprawled, rounded final *s* that is really nothing more than a hook (see Specimen 1), but can be observed in other strokes. Such a person will not be emphatic, stubborn, nor will he have a strong will.

Specimen 1

YOUNG, YOUTHFUL *e* Characteristic of youth in quality. These adjectives may be applied to a vigorous, active mind regardless of the age of the writer. When keen comprehension, optimism, and a forward sweep to the strokes revealing a vigorous mind appear in the writing, one can well deduce that the writer possesses the mental characteristics of a young person.

Specimen 2 is the writing of a "young" seventy-year-old, whose conversation is far more stimulating than that of most people half her age.

225

Specimen 2

Z

ZEALOUS *ep* Ardently devoted to a purpose; enthusiastic.
This is primarily shown in long, strong cross strokes;
such strokes reveal the writer's strong purpose and his
enthusiasm for whatever he plans to accomplish. He is
usually emotionally expressive, loyal, and determined.

At the time Specimen 1 was written, the young writer
had a zealous interest in a vocation as a nun.

Specimen 1

226

LIST OF TRAITS

The following list is composed of personality traits used in Graphoanalysis. Italicized letters indicate whether the trait is primary (p) or evaluated (e).

ACQUISITIVENESS *p*

AGGRESSIVENESS *ep*

ATTENTION TO DETAILS *p*

BLUFF *ep*

BROADMINDEDNESS *ep*

CAUTION *p*

CLANNISHNESS *p*

COLOR SENSE *p*

COMPREHENSION *p*

CONCENTRATION *p*

CONFUSION *p*

CONSERVATISM *ep*

CREATIVENESS *p*

CULTURE, DESIRE FOR *ep*

DECEIT

DECEPTIVENESS *p*

DECISIVENESS *p*

DEFIANCE *p*

DEFINITENESS *p*

DELIBERATENESS *p*

DETERMINATION *p*

DIGNITY *e*

DIPLOMACY *p*

DIRECTNESS *p*

DOMINANCE *e*

DOMINEERING NATURE *p*

EGOTISM *e*

EMOTIONAL DEPTH *p*

EMOTIONAL RESPONSIVENESS *p*

EMOTIONAL EXPRESSIVENESS *e*

ENERGY *e*

ENTHUSIASM *p*

EXAGGERATION *p*

EXPLORATORY THINKING *p*

EXTRAVAGANCE *e*

FLUIDITY *p*

FRANKNESS *p*

GENEROSITY *p*

GOAL *p*

HUMOR *p*

IDIOSYNCRACY *ep*

IMAGINATION *p*

INDECISIVENESS *p*

INDEPENDENCE *p*

INITIATIVE *p*

INSTINCTIVE THINKING *p*

INTUITION *p*

IRRITABILITY *p*

JEALOUSY *p*

JUDGMENT *ep*

LINE VALUE *p*

LITERARY ABILITY *ep*

LOGICAL THINKING *p*

LOYALTY *p*

MECHANICAL SKILL *e*

MATERIALISM *ep*

MEMORY *ep*

MUSICAL APTITUDE *ep*

OPTIMISM *p*

ORGANIZATIONAL ABILITY *ep*

OSTENTATION *ep*

PERFECTIONISM *e*

PERSISTENCE *p*

PESSIMISM *p*

PHILOSOPHY; PHILOSOPHIC IMAGINATION *p*

PHYSICAL-MINDEDNESS *p*

POISE *ep*

POSITIVENESS *p*

PRACTICAL NATURE *ep*

PRIDE *p*

PURPOSE *p*

REPRESSION *ep*

PROCRASTINATION *p*

RESENTMENT *p*

RESPONSIBILITY *p*

RETICENCE *p*

RHYTHM *p*

SARCASM *p*

SECRETIVENESS *p*

SELECTIVITY *p*

SELF-CONSCIOUSNESS *p*

SELF-CONTROL *p*

SELF-INTEREST *p*

SELFISHNESS *e*

SELF-CASTIGATION *p*

SELF-DECEIT *p*

SELF-UNDERESTIMATION *p*

SELF-RELIANCE; SELF-CONFIDENCE *p*

SENSITIVENESS *p*

SENSUALITY *p*

SENSUOUSNESS *p*

SHALLOWNESS *ep*

SHOWMANSHIP *ep*

SIMPLICITY *ep*

STINGINESS *ep*

STUBBORNNESS *p*

SUPERFICIALITY *ep*

SUPPRESSION *ep*

SUSPICION *ep*

TEMPER *p*

TENACITY *p*

TIMIDITY *e*

ULTRA-CONSERVATISM *ep*

VANITY *ep*

VARIETY, DESIRE FOR *p*

VISIONARY OUTLOOK *p*

WILL POWER *p*

WIT *e*

YIELDING NATURE *ep*